HAUNTED
SAN FRANCISCO

HAUNTED
SAN FRANCISCO

Ghost Stories from the City's Past

Compiled & Edited by

Rand Richards

Heritage House Publishers
San Francisco

Heritage House Publishers
P.O. Box 194242
San Francisco, CA 94119
E-mail: HHPRincon@aol.com

Library of Congress Cataloging-in-Publication Data

Haunted San Francisco: ghost stories from the city's past / compiled
and edited by Rand Richards.- 1st ed.
        p. cm.
Includes index.
    ISBN 1-879367-04-1
1. Ghosts–California–San Francisco. 2. Ghost
stories–California–San Francisco. I. Richards, Rand
    BF1472.U6H385 2004
    133.1'09794'61-dc22

                                2003015644

To my sister,
Lise

Contents

Preface

As someone who constantly does research on San Francisco and its history I am always coming across interesting tidbits on the City and its past. Recently I discovered a few ghost stories by 19th century authors Mark Twain and Ambrose Bierce that were set in San Francisco. It sparked my curiosity as to how many other San Francisco ghost stories there might be. As I dug deeper I was surprised to find many more than I expected. They varied quite a bit in their approaches and styles of writing. But I thought that here might be a way to approach San Francisco history from a different angle: how writers of both fiction and nonfiction have used San Francisco as a backdrop for a popular genre, the ghost story.

The stories in this anthology span nearly a century and a half, from the 1850s to the 1990s, and all use San Francisco as their setting. But the unifying entity of San Francisco ends there, inasmuch as the modes of storytelling range from journalism to investigative sleuthing to folklore to just pure fiction. The styles of writing vary too. Twenty-first century readers may find 19th century writing styles a bit antique, but that, in my view, just adds to their charm: they impart a flavor of the times in which they were written.

Some readers, because of the wide range of writing styles and topics, may find certain of the stories more to their liking than others. But I felt that it was important to show the broad range of coverage of the topic. And I hope I have provided value in republishing the works of long-deceased writers whose stories, in some cases, are seeing print here again for the first time in more than a hundred years.

Most of the stories are reprinted just as they were when first published, but in the interests of keeping the focus on the ghost parts of the story and maintaining a tight story line I have abridged a couple of the tales. Those stories in which I have made more than very minor abridgements I have noted in parentheses next to the title: (Abridged). I did no re-writing, and limited myself to correcting an occasional misspelled word that had slipped through in the original. I did not change spellings and punctuations that were common at the time, since I wanted to preserve, as much as possible, the flavor of the original copy and the words of the writers just as they wrote them. For example, although today the word street is capitalized when used after a specific street as in Market Street, in the 19th century the word street was commonly not capitalized in such usage. So I left those as is. Other examples include words such as today, which were frequently hyphenated then: to-day.

I also did not "clean up" terms that we find offensive today but that readers of a hundred years ago did not. References to Asian and other minorities reflected the times. Gelett Burgess, for example, in his story "The Ghost Extinguisher" (published in 1905), uses the word "Japs" as short for Japanese.

Since I have noted the source of each story, including the date, either at the beginning or the end, I have not included a bibliography.

Acknowledgments

Many people were helpful to me in preparing this book. I would like to start by thanking the following people and organizations for helping me ferret out some of the stories that appear herein: Susan Goldstein and Pat Akre and all the staff of the San Francisco History Center at the Main branch of the San Francisco Public Library; Patricia Keats and the Society of California Pioneers Library; Abby Bridge and the staff at the California Historical Society; and John Hawk at the Rare Book Room of Gleeson Library at the University of San Francisco.

I would also like to thank Bill Kostura for directing me to the source of several stories herein, and Chris Pollock for doing the same.

Thanks also to Elvira Monroe of Wide World Publishing/Tetra (P.O. Box 476, San Carlos, CA 94070) for permission to reprint three stories by Antoinette May from her book *Haunted Houses of California*, and to Barbara Smith and Lone Pine Publishing, both of Edmonton, Alberta, for permission to reprint four stories from *Ghost Stories of California*. A thank you as well to Rose Robinson and the University of California Press for permission to reprint "The Vanishing Hitchhiker." And I would like to thank Nina Zurier and the San Francisco Art Institute for allowing me to use Philip Kaake's photograph of the Art Institute's tower that complements the story "The San Francisco Art Institute" by Antoinette May.

A number of people gave generously of their time to review the manuscript. They are: Malcolm E. Barker of Londonborn Publications, Jeremy Lassen of Nightshade Books, Cloe Azevedo, Lindy Luoma, my sister, Lise McGrath, and my father, Robert C. Ledermann. I am

most grateful to them for their valuable comments and
suggestions.

I am also grateful to Peter Browning for his services in
helping me typeset the manuscript and for his always
sound advice on publishing matters large and small,
and to Larry Van Dyke for his patience while I dithered
over which cover design to choose from the many
options he provided.

Thanks also are due to Leonard and Priscilla Moon,
son and widow of photographer Larry Moon, for the use
of his photo of the Victorian-era stairway on the front
cover. This stairway (minus the ghost with the lamp)
appeared in several interior shots of the Alfred
Hitchcock movie *Vertigo*. The grand Victorian house
that it graced was known as the Portman Mansion (the
"McKittrick Hotel" in the movie), and stood on the
northwest corner of Gough and Eddy streets. It was
torn down in 1959 shortly after *Vertigo* was released.

Finally, I want to thank Jeff Kraft, who referred me to
Leonard Moon. I first came across Larry Moon's photo in
Jeff Kraft and Aaron Leventhal's book, *Footsteps in the
Fog: Alfred Hitchcock's San Francisco.*

Rand Richards
San Francisco
April 2004

Newspaper Stories

Sightings of and encounters with ghosts received newspaper coverage in San Francisco as early as the 1850s ("House of the Demons"). Indeed, the heyday of such reports was the latter half of the 19th century and the first few decades of the 20th century.

"House of the Demons" tells of strange and unexplained ghostly visitations that occurred in a house on Russian Hill in 1856. A detailed account of these events, written by one of the witnesses, appeared in the *Sacramento Daily Union* not long afterward. A half century later the *San Francisco Chronicle* summarized the tale in one of its Sunday editions. I have taken selections from both of these accounts to give the full flavor of what happened.

The last four articles, two each from the City's leading newspapers, the *Chronicle* and the *Examiner*, typically start off with straight reporting and end with an explanation of the mystery, with dashes of humor thrown in.

"The Kearny Street Ghost" by Mark Twain, which leads off this section, raises the question, is this story based on fact, or is it fiction?

The Kearny Street Ghost

by Mark Twain

Disembodied spirits have been on the rampage now for
more than a month past in the house of one Albert
Krum, in Kearny Street—so much so that the family find
it impossible to keep a servant forty-eight hours. The
moment a new and unsuspecting servant maid gets
fairly to bed and her light blown out, one of those dead
and damned scalliwags takes her by the hair and just
"hazes" her; grabs her by the water-fall and snakes her
out of bed and bounces her on the floor two or three
times; other disorderly corpses shy old boots at her
head, and bootjacks, and brittle chamber furniture—
washbowls, pitchers, hair-oil, teethbrushes, hoop-
skirts—anything that comes handy those phantoms
seize and hurl at Bridget, and pay no more attention to
her howling than if it were music. The spirits tramp,
tramp, tramp, about the house at dead of night, and
when a light is struck the footsteps cease and the prom-
enader is not visible, and just as soon as the light is out
that dead man goes waltzing around again. They are a
bloody lot.

The young lady of the house was lying in bed one
night with the gas turned down low, when a figure
approached her through the gloom, whose ghastly
aspect and solemn carriage chilled her to the heart.
What do you suppose she did?—jumped up and seized
the intruder?—threw a slipper at him?—"laid" him with
a misquotation from Scripture? No—none of these. But
with admirable presence of mind she covered up her
head and yelled. That is what she did. Few young
women would have thought of doing that. The ghost
came and stood by the bed and groaned—a deep,

agonizing heart-broken groan—and laid a bloody kitten on the pillow by the girl's head. And then it groaned again, and sighed, "Oh, God, and must it be?" and bet another bloody kitten. It groaned a third time in sorrow and tribulation, and went one kitten better. And thus the sorrowing spirit stood there, moaning in its anguish and unloading its mewing cargo, until it had stacked up a whole litter of nine little bloody kittens on the girl's pillow, and then, still moaning, moved away and vanished.

When lights were brought, there were the kittens, with the finger-marks of bloody hands upon their white fur—and the old mother cat, that had come after them, swelled her tail in mortal fear and refused to take hold of them. What do you think of that? what would you think of a ghost that came to your bedside at dead of night and had kittens?

Reprinted from The Golden Era, *January 28, 1866. This story was originally published in Virginia City, Nevada's* Territorial Enterprise *newspaper sometime between October 1865 and January 1866. Twain was the San Francisco correspondent for the latter paper during that period.*

It is hard to know whether Twain, who was noted for telling tall tales, based this story on something he heard or read about or whether he just made it up out of whole cloth. San Francisco city directories for the mid-1860s do not show anyone named Albert Krum, either as a resident of Kearny Street or anywhere else.

"House of the Demons"

Excerpts from "The Most Fiercely Haunted House in San Francisco," *San Francisco Chronicle*, November 9, 1902 and "Midnight Disclosures," *Sacramento Daily Union*, October 21, 23, and 24, 1856.

From the *San Francisco Chronicle*, November 9, 1902:

There are haunted houses and haunted houses. A strange light, mysterious noises, fancied visions—a murder or any other of a dozen trivial reasons—may brand a house with an evil reputation. The mere fact of neglect or desertion has given rise to tales of the marvelous. The slightest episode is sufficient excuse for the gossip to weave her webs of ghostly legend in the nooks and corners of dilapidated buildings.

A serving girl has asphyxiated herself in her upper chamber—forthwith the dwelling is said to be haunted. There are a dozen residences in the city of which tales are told, rounded upon such slim and faint foundations. Such rumors are the despair of the landlord and house agent, for as the testimony is always at fourth or fifth hand it cannot be easily refuted.

But there is one house in the city which has a history more thrilling than such hearsay fairy tales—a house where for four or five months the most extraordinary manifestations occurred by night and day time in the presence of competent, intelligent witnesses, whose evidence has been written and printed. And, moreover, these witnesses were at the time among the best-known citizens of the city, men whose characters were above reproach, whose words were never doubted. Only one of these survives, and from his recollections and the accounts printed at the time the tale is reconstructed, for forty-four years have passed since the "house of the demons" at North Beach has been visited by specters.

At the corner of Larkin and Chestnut streets there still stands [1902] a little Swiss cottage in practically the same state as it stood in September 1856. It is upon the northern spur of Russian Hill, by the reservoirs, and commands a land and water view that is perhaps the finest possible in any city in the world. The hill drops toward the west and north to Washwoman's Cove and to the upper bay, scarcely three blocks away. All Marin, Tamalpais, Alcatraz, Angel Island, Sausalito, and Belvedere look in across the channel at the little glazed piazza of the old Manrow house. The city has been settled slowly in this part of town: for North Beach, which when Meiggs[1] bought up the shore, was expected to become the chief business portion, has somehow lagged behind the rest of the waterfront. As a residence district this locality, which is sometimes called "Marathon," has only lately been built upon, but within the past few years several important residences have been erected and now its importance and beauty have been well recognized.

So the little house, so long isolated among the hills, and even yet uncrowded by neighbors, stood year after year at the extreme north end of San Francisco. Its aspect is picturesque and romantic. From house to stable a high board fence secludes the garden, and a little "Judas" wicket[2] in the door suggests a fortified enclosure. The garden is tangled and overgrown, shut in

---

1. Henry Meiggs built a wharf on the north waterfront near present-day Fisherman's Wharf in the early 1850s, but it was seldom used since most ships continued to anchor at the wharves of Yerba Buena Cove on the east waterfront.
2. A "Judas" wicket is a small door within a larger door, or a peephole.

on all sides by fences and rows of gum trees. Could one
select a stage, a place for a marvelous event to happen,
the Manrow house could not be more inspiring.

J. P. Manrow, who built the house in 1851, was one
of the best known of the pioneers. After having been
employed for several years as a civil engineer on New
York railways, he had come to California, and, in 1856,
he had a large real estate business. He was a mathema-
tician of extraordinary ability, a business man of parts,
with a clear and cool head, fine physique and a frank
and open character. He was a conspicuous figure in
town from his habit of riding with his wife and blood-
hounds all over the peninsula, and, in the eager life of
those days it was inevitable that he should become a
leader of men.

J. P. Manrow, then 40 years of age, was in the front
of the excitement of the fifties and was made judge-
advocate of the vigilance committee.[3] Among his friends
in those violent times were William H. Rhodes, an attor-
ney then contributing, under the pen name of "Caxton,"
stirring letters to the *Bulletin;* and Almarin Brooks Paul,
a mining engineer, who, with Rhodes and Washington
Bartlett, afterwards Governor of the State, was publishing the "True Californian," a daily newspaper.

The story, as told by Manrow, was one of supernatural visitations, rappings, table tippings, and so on. Spiritualism, introduced by the Fox sisters in Rochester,[4]

---

3. In 1856 several thousand of San Francisco's leading citizens
   formed an extra-legal vigilante group in response to perceived
   threats to public order. They hung several accused murderers
   and routed other criminals.
4. Spiritualism has a long history but in the U.S. it was
   kick-started on March 31, 1848 when Margarita and Catherine
   Fox of Hydesville, New York communicated with an invisible
   spirit that made rapping noises in response to questions.

had been wondered at for but fifteen or twenty years, at
that time, and everyone was interested in the subject.
But the phenomena experienced by Manrow were of a
more unusual order. There seemed to be a persistent
and malign influence connected with the house. Acts
of spite and mischief and elfish pranks were played in
broad daylight, and, when encouraged by the forming
of a "circle," these manifestations became positively
uncanny. The two young men listened, but had no
explanation to suggest, and at last they determined to
investigate the affair for themselves. To this Manrow
willingly acceded, and the night of Friday, September 19,
1856 was decided upon for the first visit for experiment.

The night of September 19th was fine, cool and lit with
a bright moon. Rhodes and Paul set out together from
the former's house on Broadway, on the south side of
Russian Hill and tramped across the hills, then
unmarred with the gashes of roads, past the slaugh-
ter-house, arriving at Manrow's house at about 8
o'clock.

The Judge had been reading up his "Icongrafia" in an
endeavor to explain the mathematical paradox or per-
petual motion machine at that time at exhibition at
Houseworth's on Clay street,[5] and the incident serves as
a reminder of the Judge's philosophic mind and scientific bias. The ladies were called down to form the circle.

Mrs. Manrow appeared with her sister, who, with a

Seances, and other attempts to communicate with the dead,
were especially popular for several decades afterward.

5. The firm of Lawrence & Houseworth was a leading photographic
    gallery that sold landscapes, portraits, and stereographs. Early
    on, they also sold optical, mathematical, and "philosophic"
    instruments, which seems to explain the reference to the
    perpetual motion machine.

daughter, had but lately come from Honolulu, and the
six sat down to the table in the library and touched
hands.

Mrs. Paul asked Mrs. Manrow if she were not frightened at what had occurred.

"No," she replied, "it was rather terrible at first, but
we're used to it now. In fact, I confess I am rather more
annoyed and indignant than terrified. These spirits, or
whatever they are, seem so childish and petulant that I
cannot understand it at all. If they were really malignant
and inflicted bodily injury for some revenge it would not
be so mysterious, but they do the most inconsequent
and silly things. Yesterday I found that all the salt had
been emptied into the sugar bowl, and all the sugar into
the salt box. And to-day I bought an expensive bonnet
downtown. When I got home I laid it upon the piano.
The next moment I turned to look at it again, and just
while my back was turned for an instant every feather
had been plucked from the bonnet! How do you explain
that?"

As soon as the circle was formed, manifestations
began to occur. Remarkable as these were, such phenomena have been described by many, and the tale of
such occurrences is threadbare. Knocks were heard in
all parts of the room, the table was raised and swung in
the air or floated a foot from the floor. But more exciting
scenes were to follow.

The lamp had been turned down part way, but the
rising moon gave the room a clear, if weak half light,
when suddenly the whole apartment was thrown into
commotion; sofa cushions were hurled in every direction, books leaped from the shelves, the doorbell was
violently rung and every person present was simultaneously struck on head or body with unseen hands.
Some had their hair pulled, some were pinched, others
kicked. During the whole of this time the members of

the company clasped hands without breaking the circuit. A book was thrown across the room and struck one of the ladies. Mr. Paul picked it up and placed it on the table. It was immediately opened; he closed it; it was opened again; and he marked the place. On turning up the light the leaf was found to contain the following sentence, the only scriptural quotation in the volume, which happened to be a book of travels: "Cannot ye discern the signs of the times?"

Mr. Manrow now proposed that the spirits should wake up a negro servant who slept in the stable, and hardly had this been mentioned, when, terrified out of his senses, the man burst open the stable door with a shriek and rushed in his nightshirt down the walk toward the library window. He broke into the kitchen, and immediately the group of watchers in the window perceived a horrible form appear from the ground in front of them.

From the Sacramento Daily Union, *October 21, 1856, William Rhodes narrating:*

This terrible apparition was the most frightful figure that ever the human eye beheld. Language is utterly inadequate to describe it. There it reclined in the clear moonlight, silent, still, and sublime in its horrible deformity. If all the fiends in hell had combined their features into one master-piece of ugliness and revolting hideousness of countenance, they could not have produced a face so full of horrors. It was blacker than the blackest midnight that ever frowned in starless gloom over the storm-swept ocean.

Over its head and body it had spread a mantle of the most stainless white. It looked like a robe of new fallen snow covering the blackened remains of a conflagration. It seemed as though personified sin had snatched the garment of a seraph as he floated by, and spread it over its thunder-scarred and hell-scorched form. Its face was turned toward us in profile, and I saw upon its features an expression of cruelty and revenge, darkened by the frown of everlasting despair. Hope never sat there.

We all sprang towards the window and gazed in petrified astonishment and horror at the loathsome goblin—for surely there was but little of human in it, except the form. My first impulse was to get out of the house into the open air. I rushed through the door, followed by the rest of the company except for Mr. Paul, who still maintained his position at the window, and scanned the phantom with close and critical scrutiny. As we left the room a new manifestation occurred. Chairs, tables, rugs, pokers and cushions seemed to be imbued with vitality, and danced before us with the most admired disorder. As I passed out, a cushion was thrown from the parlor, in which a light was burning, and struck me on the head. At the same moment, one of the ladies was struck with a chair covering and almost blinded with the dust. I stepped into the parlor, but it was utterly vacant. I then went to the front door and attempted to open it, but much to the astonishment of us all, the front gate had been torn loose, and brought some ten or twelve steps, and placed so as to barricade the door and prevent it from swinging open. Unable to get out in this direction, I followed Mr. Manrow and the ladies, who rushed through the back entry, and tried to intercept the apparition at the kitchen door. But when we reached the door, and opened it, the goblin was invisible. It had disappeared as suddenly as it appeared.

We agreed at once to dispense with the presence of that hideous phantom, and to strive to call up the spirits of the beautiful and good, whose forms would dispel the remembrance of the vision just vanished.

We had scarcely composed ourselves at the table, and made known our wishes, when we received unequivocal promises that our desires should be gratified. All at once, I felt a cool, delicate hand playing with my hair, and gently stroking my cheeks and forehead. At the same moment a similar phenomenon was observed by all present at the circle. Each one felt the same soft hands pressing their brows, cheeks and hair. What rendered this manifestation so surprising was the fact we held each other tightly by the hands, forming an unbroken circle, so as to prevent the possibility of fraud or deception. At this moment, Mr. Paul announced that he could distinctly see the hands as they flitted about the table in every possible direction. Hardly had he spoken before I myself beheld them; at first very indistinctly, but gradually and more palpably, until at the expiration of five or six minutes, I beheld the spirit hands quite as plainly as though they had been of ordinary flesh and blood. It is impossible to say, with any certainty, how many of these hands were floating in the atmosphere at the same moment; there were certainly as many as a dozen, and possibly many more. We were all touched in different parts of the body, at one and the same time, and the expressions, "how gentle!" "how soft!" "how soothing!" escaped constantly from all our lips.

Indeed, the influence of these caressing hands was as pleasant and loving as the effect of the horrible appearance of the Goblin had been revolting. The good spirits seemed to be striving to make amends for the pain and sorrow we had experienced, by soothing all our fears and quieting all nervous excitement. Mr. Manrow, who had been suffering all the evening from severe toothache, brought on by severe cold, requested these gentle beings to cure his tooth and relieve him from pain. At once, several of them commenced manipulating the outer surface of the jaw, and continued to do so until the uneasiness was entirely removed and a perfect cure effected.

Satisfied with the wonderful phenomena we had witnessed, and soothed and delighted almost beyond measure by the kind messages given us by those purported to be our guardian spirits, we very reluctantly broke up the circle and returned home, where we arrived at the early hour of one o'clock Saturday morning.

The following evening, a clear and moonlit night, Almarin Brooks Paul and William Rhodes returned to the Manrow house. This time new spirits made their appearance.

From the Sacramento Daily Union, *October 23, 1856:*

The moon had by this time arisen, and was shining so brightly that every object in the yard could be seen quite clearly and identified. Suddenly Mr. Paul sprang to his feet, and declared that he beheld the phantom approaching the window from a north-easterly direction. Our attention was immediately directed toward that spot, and there, sure enough, it stood—with the rays of the moon falling full and clear upon it. It was of an entirely different form and figure from the terrible apparition of the evening previous, and if the truth must be told, I must confess that I for one was excessively glad that it was so. I never desire to behold that hideous demon again. The one we now beheld was seemingly a girl about 10 or 12 years old. She approached us in a stooping attitude, and flitted back and forth, close to the window, several times before she entirely disappeared.

No sooner had she done so, however, than another spirit made its appearance *right at the window,* and within six feet of the circle. At this, Mrs. Manrow's nerves entirely gave way, and she uttered a loud scream. The phantom, apparently hearing this, flitted away towards the kitchen, and instead of entering by the door, which, however, was closed, passed easily through the solid side of the house, and remained several seconds inside. Presently, it came forth again, as it entered, and stood half inside, and half out at the same moment; the thick planking and plastering, forming not the slightest obstruction to its passage in and out. This was repeated several times, until we all became perfectly satisfied of the supernatural character of the apparition, and then it flitted off, and was lost in the surrounding atmosphere. The appearance of this spirit was different from either of the others. It was extremely tall and thin, and resembled a shadow more than a substance. It was, however, in the human form, though gigantic in its height. Neither the face of this spirit nor that of the preceding one was visible, or at least was not observed by any of the circle. For my own part, I was too easily engaged in watching its maneuvers, to criticize very clearly its features. That anything wearing the human form should possess the power of appearing and disappearing at pleasure, should flit back and forth, like the phantasmagoria of a magic lantern, and above all, should actually enter the house, and come out of it by passing directly through the planking and wall, afforded food enough for the thought, without the desire of augmenting the wonder by a very critical scrutiny of the countenance.

The last experiment of the evening was what is denominated a physical demonstration. Mr. Paul had several times been upset in his chair and tumbled upon the floor, by these invisible visitors; indeed, he found it impossible to occupy a chair in a certain remote corner, it being at the same time out of the reach of any person in the room. Finally, as a last test of their power, we demanded that he be lifted up and tossed upon the table. Almost as quick as thought, he was raised out of

his chair, and the next moment we beheld him sprawl-
ing at full length on the table at which we were sitting,
and from which none of us had moved. In his attempt to
account for this wonderful trick, he says that all he distinctly recollects about it was, that something grasped
him by the collar of the coat, whilst something else lifted
him from the floor; that then he was lunged forward,
and finally hurled at full length upon the table. He made
no resistance, for the simple reason that, before he
thought of resisting, the whole affair was over, and the
experiment completed. He was not hurt by the fall,
although he came down with a force that told no great
circumspection had been taken to render his cherry
plank couch a bed of down.

In rising, he appeared awkward and ridiculous
enough to satisfy his worst enemy. The expression of his
face was anything but pleasing or philosophical, as the
portion of his body had been anything but genteel or
graceful.

Thus terminated, more than an hour after midnight,
the phenomena of the second night.

From the Sacramento Daily Union, *the third and final night,
October 24, 1856:*

After sitting for some moments in perfect stillness
and silence, we heard something underneath the
book-case, standing in the northeast corner of the room,
and distant some ten or twelve feet from any member of
the circle. The noise became more and more audible and
distinct, until finally several large maps, which had been
rolled up and placed there for security, were taken up
violently and thrown several feet towards the center of
the room. And here I may remark that the room in
which we sat was only partially darkened, the candle
being placed in the piazza, and its light shining full into

the chamber. Immediately after the maps were removed, one of the large globes, which was occupying a recess underneath the book-case, started from its position, and rolled itself along upon its legs, until it came close to the table, from which none of us had stirred. It then deliberately passed along underneath the table, and came out at the opposite side, being capsized just as it issued forth. Almost contemporaneously with this the other globe started off from its moorings, and passed along towards the opposite window, in full view of all of us. Just before reaching the window it increased its speed and was dashed against one of the lower panes, and with such violence that the glass was broken. After the conclusion of these experiments, we signified our desire to behold once more the forms of our spiritual visitants.

We were not doomed to disappointment; for on casting our eyes in the indicated direction, there it flitted like a will-o-the-wisp, right before us.

This light had a very peculiar appearance. When I first beheld it, it presented the same aspect as a large globe lantern. The light, however, was wavy, and it did not cast any shadow. Gradually it approached, close up to the window, then it receded as slowly, at the same moment changing its circular shape to an oblong and irregular figure. Then it flitted from one side to another, and back again, its form undergoing curious and perplexing changes all the time. Then it withdrew some distance from the house, and assumed a new shape altogether.

Mr. Paul at this instant fell upon the floor, and placing his eyes very close to the glass window, declared that he could see it much more distinctively, and that it was again modifying its appearance. It next assumed the precise shape of a newly made grave. There it lay, close upon the ground, about six feet long, with the same rounded and heaped up figure, shining with a pale glare, brighter than the moon, but entirely without any resplendence. It lit up nothing near it, cast no shadow, and seemed more like a brilliant phosphor, than any flame produced by heat. It did not continue in this guise very long; but soon transformed into a thin, narrow line, stretching several feet along the ground, and gradually melting entirely away.

The inquiry very naturally arises in this place, whether or not it was possible for any human being with a magic lantern in his hand, to have produced a similar phenomenon? Without a moment's hesitation, I answer, No. There were some peculiarities about this light which no skill, however great, could have contrived, in the first place, it must be remembered that it approached to within a few feet of the window, and flitted back and forth, changing its form every moment and gradually lengthening itself out, until it presented the perfect outline of a grave. Evidently this appearance could not have been produced, so close at hand, without our seeing the machinery employed in the deception. For the night was not dark, and the eye could trace distinctly the form of every tree, bush and object in the vicinity. And, secondly, no artifice could have produced a meteor of such peculiar appearance. The luminary did not look at all like those bright and evanescent gleams which we sometimes see shooting athwart the darkness, but it presented to the vision a full, distinct and sharp volume, much more brilliant than moonlight, and yet not so red and fiery as the rays of a torch.

In concluding this series of papers, on this most curious of modern mysteries, I cannot refrain from expressing the hope that J. P. Manrow will favor the public with a full account of the events which have been transpiring at his house for the past four or five months. His known scientific character, his reputation for truth and veracity, and above all, his steadiness of nerve under

circumstances that would appall even the most coura-
geous, eminently fit him to be no less the observer than
the recorder of those terrific and inexplicable phenomena. Scenes have been related to me by him which, if
witnessed by ordinary men, would have sent them to the
hospital or asylum; scenes which would startle the souls
of the most philosophic, even to hear related, and would
dwell in the minds of the sensitive and nervous person
forever; scenes, in short, which, whatever may be said of
the agencies employed in producing them, especially
deserve to be recorded as a portion of the history of the
time, and spread before the scientific and learned world
for their instruction and solution.

*The "House of the Demons," isolated as it was from other
dwellings, was spared the flames of the 1906 fire. The house
occupied the northeast corner of Chestnut and Larkin streets.
Standing on the site today are the 1927 13-story co-op at 1090
Chestnut and the 19-story high rise at 1080 Chestnut, which
was erected in 1961. (The address of the "House of Demons"
was 1098 Chestnut Street.)*

From the *San Francisco Chronicle*, November 9, 1902.

From the *San Francisco Chronicle,* December 10, 1871:

THREE PHANTOMS

The North Beach Ghost Mystery

Another Man's Head and a Butterfly Discovered

FULL PARTICULARS AND PORTRAITS OF THE SHADOWS ON WINDOWS

The "Chronicle's" Theory of the Phenomena—
Intense Excitement—
Thousands of People Visit the Scene—
The First Ghost Purchased by a Showman

Editor's Note: The previous day's Chronicle *had a brief article about the "Mason Street Specter." By the following day it had become a phenomenon calling for front-page treatment.*

The town was greatly excited yesterday over the spectral figure on the Mason-street window, and during the day thousands of people thronged to the locality to get a sight at the new sensation. In yesterday's CHRONICLE we gave a brief description of the apparition, but as two similar figures have made their appearance in the neighborhood, a recapitulation of the whole story will not be uninteresting. Ghost No. 1,

THE OLD ORIGINAL GHOST,

made its appearance, as stated yesterday, about four or five days ago, on one of the second-story windows of No. 2119 Mason street, between Lombard and Chestnut. The house is tenanted by a Swedish widow named

Jorgenson, whose husband died a little over a year ago while revisiting his native place. Madame Jorgenson, in a private interview with a CHRONICLE reporter, stated she had had a good deal of trouble lately, chiefly from relatives in regard to pecuniary matters. On Monday she was told by some children that there was a man's face in the window. She went to the upper room, on the window of which the face was said to be, but saw nothing. She then went into the street, and plainly saw what appeared to be a photograph of

A MAN'S FACE

on the glass. Scarcely crediting the evidence of her own senses, she called several neighbors to witness the marvelous apparition. The news spread like wildfire, and curiosity-seekers, idlers, reporters and the public generally flocked in crowds to the spot, until the street for a block was nearly impassable. The image remained visible during the whole time, without apparent change, and great was the impression produced by it on the spectators. As to the image of

"HER DECEASED HUSBAND,"

which an evening journal mentioned as appearing to Mrs. Jorgenson, we have the testimony of that lady herself to the contrary. The room in which the specter-bearing window stands is small and contains a picture and a looking-glass among the rest of the articles of furniture. Therefore there is no object which might produce on the window the reflection of a human face.

Among the wondering assemblage in front of the house, many and various were the speculations indulged in as to the probable cause of the phenomenon. Every man had a favorite theory of his own, and clung to it with commendable tenacity.

At half-past 11 o'clock yesterday morning the landlord

of the house came with a view of purchasing the window. He first offered $2,500, but immediately repented
and offered $25. His generosity was not appreciated, and
the mysterious visitor remained unsold.

R. B. WOODWARD

came shortly afterward to negotiate for the purchase of
it for the "Gardens."[1] The frame in which is the image
was then taken out for Mr. Woodward's inspection. At
his request it was taken to the office of Judge Sawyer,
on Clay street, where it remained until 6 o'clock last
evening, when Mr. Woodward having purchased it for
$250, had it transported to the Gardens, where it will be
on exhibition to-day. Prior to its removal from Judge
Sawyer's office the CHRONICLE'S special artist was
afforded an opportunity of making

AN ACCURATE SKETCH

of the mysterious picture, which is here appended for
the gratification of our reader's curiosity.

The image is of life-size, and seems to be that of a
rather handsome man, with mustache and goatee; hair
parted in the middle and waving off the forehead. The
eyes are quite distinct, and, from a circular rim beneath
each, seem to be spectacled. The expression of the countenance is thoughtful and rather sad. The head is pen-
sively cast on the left shoulder, the outlines of which are
visible. The hair is quite well defined, and a lock seems
parted from the rest and falling naturally over the forehead. The image can only be seen by reflected light, and
is best apparent when the glass is held at an angle of 45
degrees to the luminary source. Viewed from a short

---

1. The "Gardens" was Woodward's Gardens, a popular amusement
   park that was located in the Mission District. Robert B.
   Woodward was the owner.

Ghost Number One.

distance it appears to be the reflection of a human face, or rather a not well-developed negative. Viewed closely it is perceived to be simply iridescence, such as is frequently seen on window-glasses, and which is the combined result of dust and moisture.

GHOST NUMBER TWO.

About 2 o'clock yesterday afternoon a couple of school girls noticed a similar apparition on a window in the house of J. J. Hucks, of axle-grease fame, No. 708 Lombard street.[2] Immediately was raised a hue and cry, and the house was surrounded. This second apparition is far more vivid than the first, but the features are not so regular. The side of the house on which it is, faces directly west. The apparition is of an elderly gentleman, with very grotesque features. He presents a profile view, and is looking contemplatively upward. The pane of glass is rather small, and the old gentleman's head seems to be squeezed in, regardless of comfort. We took a careful sketch on the spot:

At this point of the proceedings Mr. Hucks came out, and was terribly wrothy. He asked of us who and what

---

2. Number 708 Lombard Street is between Mason Street and Columbus Avenue. The Victorian house that stood there then was the home of John J. Hucks, a partner in the firm of Hucks, Lambert & Greene, manufacturers of axle grease and dealers in rosin and lubrication oils.

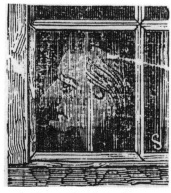

Ghost Number Two.

we were; and on hearing our business, broke out violently, declaring that he "wanted no such d——d thing as that put in the CHRONICLE about his house." We were inexorable, however, and the storm blew over. But just as we had finished our sketch the blinds of the window were drawn down violently, and the ghost disappeared.

We understand that since then the specter has improved considerably in appearance, and has straightened his nose and turned out side-whiskers and mustache. He was clean-shaven when we saw him, and his nose was of the

BOTTLE-GOURD TYPE.

We congratulate him on his cultivating "style." About 4 o'clock R. B. Woodward visited Mr. Hucks with a view of investment. Mr. Woodward evidently considers the ghost business lucrative, for he is buying up the market. Owing to the fact of his being early in the season, specters command a fair price—$250 being paid for this one.

GHOST NUMBER THREE.

Just as Ghost No. 2 "vanished into air" we heard loud shoutings on Mason street, and carried along by the throng found ourselves in front of house No. 2109 Mason street,[3] a few doors above the house in which Phantom 1 was holding forth. Ghost No. 3 was a curiosity. It assumed the shape of a butterfly, the outlines of which

3. Number 2109 Mason St. was between Lombard and Chestnut.

were perfect. The wings were spotted in the center and tailed out in the end like those of the *lepidoptua*. The beautiful little *papilio* is nearest in nature:

What the object of any spirit may be in assuming the shape of a butterfly, we can't see, unless it is to make a

Ghost Number Three.

poor reporter overhaul numerous huge volumes of entomology, for the purpose of finding out the particular caterpillar he comes from. Ghost No. 3 faded away shortly, and gradually disappeared. We heard a report current this evening that he had again shown himself, but in a *different form!* As to the truth of this, we have not been able to ascertain.

MORE GHOSTS.

About 3 o'clock P.M. a man came rushing down Mason street, with one boot off, and reported *another* ghost on the southeast corner of Mason and Green. But we had our fill of specters. It was getting rather monotonous this ghost business. So we determined not to interview this fourth abomination. For a recent introduction the ghost business is quite a success, and we congratulate Mr. Woodward on the honor he has of entertaining these spiritual visitants.

ADDITIONAL ITEMS.

The rush being temporarily checked by the announcement that Ghost No. 1 was dethroned, the Superintendent of the North Beach and Mission Railroad went yesterday, at 4 o'clock, to Mrs. Jorgenson to negotiate for his Ghostship's reinstatement. The North Beach and Mission R. R. were making a good thing out of it, and the Superintendent is not to be blamed. His visit, however, was fruitless, as Mr. Woodward had already secured the prize and trundled it off. To-day is the benefit of the Mission-street cars.

MARKET QUOTATION.

"Ghosts in good supply, but prices firm." We quote prime at \$200@\$250; interior do., \$90@\$100.

A SOLUTION OF THE MYSTERY.

As already stated, iridescent formations—the combined result of dust and moisture—on window panes are frequently observed. This leads at once to the true solution of the mystery. In our opinion it is simply an ordinary iridescent spot of collection of spots, resembling in the eye of fancy a human face; but we do not deny that it may be a sort of photograph of a real image. It may be this, and

COULD EASILY BE FORMED.

For instance, if a man, heated and perspiring, were to approach his face near a cold glass, the moisture arising from the fleshy parts would condense on its surface in tolerably accurate relative position, and, with any dust on the glass, form a deposit which would leave an iridescent stain. The hair, beard, eyebrows, etc., not exuding any moisture, would not form such a deposit on the glass, and consequently would be represented by absence of iridescent matter. Now this is actually the case with the picture in question. The cheeks, throat, forehead, nose, etc., are, on close examination, seen to be iridescent spots, while the beard, eyebrows, hair, etc., are plainly the ordinary surface of the glass.

The article concluded with examples of non-ghostly iridescence and explained how those effects were realized. For

two or three days afterward the following ad appeared in the Chronicle, *then stopped:*

    On the site of all the locations mentioned, which are just to
the northwest of today's North Beach Playground, now stand
post-1906 construction. The "haunted" houses that were the
subject of this article when it appeared in 1871 were most
likely consumed by the 1906 fire.

From the *San Francisco Examiner*, May 15, 1893:

WAS HAUNTED LONG AGO

Story of a Post-Street Building
That Has Ever Been Vacant

THE HOUSE WITHOUT A DOOR

**Why Dan O'Connell Would Never Pass
That Way—A $5,000 Place That Has
Waited Thirty Years for a Tenant**

Blackened and lonesome-looking is the structure—a house without a doorway—that has stood for seventeen years at 924 Post street, just below the Larkin-street corner. It would be called an old house on account of its abandoned appearance, but only thirty years have passed since transpired the first events in its mysterious history. Nobody has ever stayed for a night within its walls, and people say that if the house eventually becomes a place of abode it will be when a second change of its location shall have broken the secret spell.

The house is haunted—if ever there was a ghost on top of the earth, and if Dan O'Connell, Prince of Bohemia, knows what he has been afraid of since he landed on these foreign shores.[1] Those who have seen

---

1. The reference to "Dan O'Connell, Prince of Bohemia" probably points to a journalist of the time by that name who resided at the Bohemian Club, then at 130 Post Street. The unnamed writer of this article surely knew Dan O'Connell and seems to have enjoyed teasing his superstitious colleague.

the O'Connell make a detour of several blocks when he merely wanted to pass that section of the street may understand the reason now, if they never knew it before.

BUILT AND ABANDONED.

It was in the early 60s that the house was erected on a site somewhere near the corner of Post and Larkin streets—the exact place is forgotten and so is the name of the original owner. The edifice was finished only on the exterior, owing to some strange family misfortune, and so it stood for thirteen years. A purchaser finally moved it to the recent location, but inability to keep up the payments resulted in loss of both house and land. Since then a real-estate dealer has had possession of the property. Nobody venturesome enough to occupy it has been found, however, and the walls have remained exactly as the builder left them. The latest chapter is the removal of the building to Fulton and Divisadero streets, where a man whose name is Campbell and who doesn't believe in spooks proposes to plaster the rooms and make his home therein.

Originally the house must have cost close upon $5,000. It is two and a half stories high, with pointed roof, and in addition to the main portion there is a large wing. The timber is the very best and experts say that the house is practically as good to-day, from their standpoint, as it was when erected. There is an unusual amount of builders' ornamentation on the unpainted exterior, but within are the dreary and unlathed walls and not even a stairway. Glass once filled the windows, but the throwing propensities of boys who thereabouts grew up into greater lines of usefulness long ago compelled the substitution of heavy oaken boards.

Strangest of all the strange circumstances, the house has not a door. Go around it whatever way you will and you will find but the windows and the empty window sashes. That can be explained only as a freak of the builder, who ignored the common plan of street stairways and had an entrance through the floor from a brick basement.

O'CONNELL AND THE SPIRITS.

Of course there is a reason for the long neglect of so good a bit of property, and as the story was told to O'Connell it is that the house has always been haunted. Whether the ghostly manifestations still continue is not known, for nobody has looked within the house at night for more than fifteen years, but in former times there were few there acquainted with the circumstances who doubted the supernatural occupancy. Loud wailings of an old man were heard and there were apparitions of a gray-haired woman, through whose phosphorescent form the unlathed walls and the uncouth chimney could be seen. A beautiful maiden didn't figure in this case at all. Once an appalling clatter was heard just after midnight, as if the whole house was tumbling down into the cellar, but the next morning not a vestige of debris could be found. It was said afterward that a couple of medical students had caused tumult by carelessly letting a newly prepared skeleton fall headlong down from the garret, but Dan O'Connell would never accept such a nonsensical theory as that.

After the house was finally abandoned and the heavy oaken covering of the windows concealed the specters from view the midnight orgies were still heard. Gradually the disturbance ceased as demand for the house was lessened, and so it was suspected that the ghosts were in some way connected with the original ownership and their only object in haunting the place was to prevent tenants from occupying it.

THE DESERTED HOUSE TO PROVE IT.

This is the story as it was told to Dan O'Connell, and as it has always commanded the respect of that mortal. No explanation of the ghosts' existence has been demanded, the O'Connell being satisfied to reason from the effect that there must have been some deplorable cause. If anybody doubted or questioned why he avoided that region there was the dark, deserted building and there were the people who had heard the cries.

To-day the building stands at the corner of Polk and Ellis streets, in the middle of the pavement. It is on the road for the second time, and in a few days, if the spirits are willing, it will stand on its third foundation at Divisadero and Fulton streets. Mr. Campbell bought the really valuable structure for $17. He is to pay $400 for the removal, and if he will transform one of the windows into a door, plaster the rooms, buy a lot of glass and do considerable painting, then he will have a good-looking and commodious house. If the spooks stay away he ought to be happy, but he will never get Dan O'Connell to call on him.

No structure in the vicinity of Divisadero and Fulton streets today resembles the one pictured here.

From the *San Francisco Chronicle,* January 6, 1908:

PARK GHOST HOLDS UP AUTOMOBILE PARTY

Police Are Asked to Run Down Spook Who Terrorized Motorists

WOMEN SHRIEK IN FRIGHT

Confident That Spectral Visitor Tried To Block Their Progress

The park police have been asked to arrest a ghost. The spectral visitor to the city's big playground blocked the passage of an automobile owned by Arthur Pigeon, the cement man, just before dawn yesterday morning, and had several of the women occupants of the machine in a state bordering on hysteria.

According to Pigeon, the thing stood directly in front of the speeding automobile, clad in a luminous white robe, and holding its arm extended as though to stop the progress of the machine. It was first seen by one of the women occupants of the machine. She emitted a shriek of terror, and Pigeon, who was at the tiller, looked to one side of the south drive. What he saw caused him to send the machine ahead at full speed.

The auto sped at its best clip for nearly half a mile, when it was overtaken and stopped by Mounted Policeman D. A. Daly. He commanded the occupants to stop, and they did so reluctantly. All of them were wide-eyed and shaking with terror.

"We were held up by a ghost," gasped Pigeon.

Policeman Daly, to whom the Park at night has no terrors, smiled knowingly. He even insinuated that a visit to beach resorts might produce ghosts or spirits.

But Pigeon insisted that the automobile had been held up by something supernatural. The policeman suggested that the party go back to the place where the ghost was seen and point it out. He guaranteed that the spook would spend the night in jail. At the very thought the feminine occupants of the machine shrieked aloud. They would not return to the place under any consideration.

Finally Pigeon volunteered to guide the officer to the place.

The other occupants of the automobile dismounted hastily, and Pigeon slowly ran back to the place where he had seen the supernatural visitor, the policeman riding at the side of the machine and ready to try the remonstrative powers of the regulation police revolver should anything in white appear. When they arrived at the spot where the spook stood, the dawn was breaking. Pigeon pointed to a tall cypress tree and whispered, "There is where it was, right in front of that tree."

Policeman Daly cantered over to the tree with his revolver in his hand. Nothing like a ghost challenged his approach, and he rode back to Pigeon, still convinced that the visitation was merely the result of a visit to the beach resorts.

"It was a thin, tall figure in white," declared Pigeon, "and it seemed to shine. It had long, fair hair and was barefooted. I did not notice the face. I was too frightened and too anxious to get away from the place."

All of the members of the auto party stick to the same sort of story. They are convinced that they had seen a ghost, and were only too anxious to get out of the Park. Captain Gleeson of the Park Station was informed of the affair and gave orders that any ghost answering this description is to be arrested on sight. The tale has made an impression on some of the men, and none of them are over-anxious for the detail of bringing in Pigeon's ghost.

From the *San Francisco Examiner*, May 11, 1914:

PISH! COLONY OF SPOOKS IN PARK

Cigarette Smoking Ghosts, With Cat They Torture and Queer Bulldog in Quigley House

The ghosts have crossed the bay.

Heretofore all the spooks have played around Oakland and Berkeley, where they have entertained an appreciative and select few, who in turn thrilled the populace with stories of their experiences.

San Francisco's ghosts occupy the old Quigley house in the gully of Golden Gate Park near Frederick Street.[1] It has always been a place of gloom and mystery. Six or seven persons have died there, and for years the house has been deserted.

GHOSTS MOVE IN.

Curiously enough, the haunted house, always quiet and forbidding in its deserted silence, has been shunned by everybody until within the last two weeks, when the ghosts moved in. Within two weeks hundreds of brave young men have visited the haunted house, swearing to solve the mystery.

It is a conventional ghost family that occupies the house, the old-fashioned kind that drags heavy chains

---

1. Patrick Quigley was a long-time employee and foreman of Golden Gate Park who lived alone in a small house in the park near present-day Kezar Stadium until his death in 1912.

over the floors, moans at the moon and keeps a cat,
which it tortured into unhallowed wails.

The credit for discovering such an entertaining colony
of spooks is said to belong to William Neeson, who owns
a cigar store at Waller and Stanyan streets; Joseph and
Lloyd McLaughlin and Paul Devine, all living in the
neighborhood of Waller and Stanyan.

FIREMEN TAKE TO HEELS.

Their first vivid accounts of the ghost were flouted by
the brave and intelligent residents of the park region.

Finally several firemen from Engine Co. 40, Waller
and Stanyan streets, were induced to visit the place.
They walked boldly through the rooms on the ground
floor, and James Clowe and James Phipps began to
climb the dark stairs. Then the chains began to rattle,
and an unearthly groan came from above. The firemen
retreated.

Merwin Rudie, student at the Affiliated Colleges[2] was
the next to investigate. He was accompanied by other
students and a professor from the Affiliated Colleges.
They came on a quest of science, and stayed even in the
face of hair raising groans and rattling chains.

Rudie took a piece of pasteboard and wrote on it:
"Who are you?"

Then he tossed it upstairs. The pasteboard came fly-
ing downstairs again accompanied by groans. There
were mysterious hieroglyphics on the card. The faculty
members and students of psychology have been

---

2. Affiliated Colleges were departments of the University of
    California's San Francisco campus. They were located on
    Parnassus Avenue between First and Third avenues, just a
    few blocks south of Golden Gate Park.

devoting their spare hours since to deciphering the hieroglyphics.

SPOOKS SMOKE CIGARETTES.

The ghosts entertained a crowd of about fifty last night. Dudley Chase, 1112 Eleventh Avenue, found things so terrifying he fainted.

Only one man refused to stretch his legs with the forty-nine who ran. This straggler stayed behind, walked up stairs where he found two ghosts smoking cigarettes. They were sitting on covered tin tubs. The floor was strewn with small stones.

The ghosts showed the visitors some of their tricks. The tin cans had bolts and stones in them, and when they were rolled over the floor, they made an ominous racket resembling the rattling of chains.

In one corner was a muzzled bulldog, that never uttered a sound when an ill humored alley cat was led up to him and began to wail and spit. Then the ghosts left.

Less than a week after the "ghosts" were unmasked, the Quigley house burned down, possibly due to arson.

Haunted Houses and Ships

Haunted houses and ships, and the ghosts who supposedly inhabit them, have proved fertile ground for writers for generations. Here are five stories by two contemporary authors that are bound together by eerie happenings in various San Francisco locations.

Northern California writer Antoinette May tells of strange goings-on at three San Francisco locations— "The Haskell House" at Ft. Mason, and "The San Francisco Art Institute" and "The Montandon Townhouse," both on Russian Hill. A psychical researcher, she conducted investigations and interviewed people who told her of their ghostly encounters.

Canadian writer (from Edmonton, Alberta) Barbara Smith, with over a dozen books of ghost stories to her credit, tells the story in "Murder So Foul" of the *Squando*, a 19th-century sailing ship haunted by the ghost of its murdered first mate. This section concludes with her tale "Ghostly Lifesaver," in which an apparition rowing a small boat suddenly appears in the middle of the Pacific Ocean and saves the lives of two shipwrecked men.

The Haskell House (Abridged)

by Antoinette May

(Editor's Note: U.S. Senator David C. Broderick was mortally wounded in a duel near Lake Merced with southerner David S. Terry on September 12, 1859. The anti-slavery Broderick stayed at the Haskell House, aka "Quarters Three," at Ft. Mason before the duel and was brought back there afterward where he died three days later.)

Over the years a succession of tenants, military officers, have complained that the place (the Haskell House) was haunted. A man in a long black coat with a top hat has been seen many times pacing back and forth. Could this be Broderick reliving his anguish on the night before the duel? Many people have thought so.

Colonel Cecil Puckett, who lived in the house during the late 1970s, told of a presence in the kitchen. "I feel that something or someone follows me about the house at times," he said, "I even feel that it watches me in the shower."

Subsequent tenants continued to feel a presence. Capt. Jim Knight, (ret.) a recent MTMC[1] Western Area deputy commander who lived in the house for two years, was certain that the house was haunted. "There's no doubt about it," he stated. "We didn't see or hear anything, but sometimes we'd be in the kitchen and the lights in the dining room would go on by themselves. Or we'd be downstairs and the john in the bathroom upstairs would flush by itself."

---

1. The Military Traffic Management Command is responsible for moving troops, cargo, household goods, vehicles, and so forth to their various destinations.

More eerie occurrences happened to Capt. Everett Jones, (ret.) who succeeded Knight in Quarters Three and lived there for three and a half years.

"After we moved in we had a couple of parties there and we joked about a ghost being in the house," Jones recalled. "One Saturday morning after a party, I was in the kitchen putting things away and heard a big crash. Upon investigating, I found that a picture with a picture hook and a nail an inch-and-a-half long had crashed to the floor. It didn't look like the nail had pulled out; it looked like someone had pushed it from behind.

"There was a similar incident later when five pictures fell off the same wall," Knight continued. "And my daughter was sitting on her bed one morning and one of those bolt-on light fixtures fell off without warning.

"There was no earthquake to account for it either," Knight added. "That all happened in the first six months after we moved in—we stopped joking about the ghost after that."

Capt. James W. Lunn, MTMC Western Area's present deputy commander, and his family live in Quarters Three now [c.1990]. Captain Lunn tells of going over to the house to check it out before moving in. "One of the painters said that he'd been working on the windows one day and *something* pushed him right out!"

Later the Lunn family saw plants tip over by themselves and shadows move across empty rooms. "Often I hear footsteps when I'm home alone," he said. "The dog pricks up her ears and runs to look—she hears them too—but we don't see anything."

Sylvia Brown, (a psychic) while investigating the house, saw clairvoyantly a whole mosaic of spirits. First there was a man in a long black coat with a top hat who paced back and forth. Could that have been Broderick?

Then Sylvia described black people hiding in the cellar. "They were hidden there for their own protection, but many of them were frightened and unhappy, uncertain of the future," she explained.

Considering the state of San Francisco politics in the 1850s, this seems highly probable. Surely Haskell, an anti-slavery crony of Broderick's, would have aided fugitives even to the extent of hiding them if necessary in his home.

Those turbulent times have left their imprint on the pretty two-story house where many dramatic events have taken place over the years.

Of course it's haunted.

Quarters Three, the historic Haskell House, is located at Fort Mason at the foot of Franklin Street in San Francisco.

Reprinted from Haunted Houses of California *(1990) by Antoinette May, with the kind permission of Wide World Publishing/Tetra.*

The Haskell House. Photograph by Rand Richards.

The San Francisco Art Institute

by Antoinette May

Can unfulfilled longings trigger a ghost into being?

A group of prominent psychics hold frustrated creativity to blame for a series of hauntings that have mystified faculty and students at the San Francisco Art Institute.

The Institute is a splendid example of the Spanish Colonial revival architecture popular during the 1920's. The walls are stripped concrete dyed a soft adobe ocher, the roofs red tile. A bell tower rises above the patio in the manner of an early mission.

"There's something strange about the bell tower," students began to whisper almost immediately after the Institute opened its doors on January 15, 1927. But it was twenty years before anything really happened.

Artist Bill Morehouse is now a professor in the art department at Sonoma State College, but in 1947 he was a night watchman and student at the Institute. To reduce expenses, he decided to sleep in the tower.

He vividly recalls his first night there. "It was around midnight and I had gone to bed on the third level. I heard the doors opening and closing down below. I'd locked them myself, but I assumed that it was the janitor, so I didn't bother to investigate. I listened to the footsteps climbing to the first level, then to the second and finally to the third.

"The doorknob turned and the door to my room opened and closed as though someone had entered. It was a large room and well lighted. Inside were a water tank, my bedroll and me. I saw no one but heard footsteps passing through the room, turning, then walking back to the door. The knob turned, the door opened and closed and the footsteps continued up to the observation platform."

That was Morehouse's first encounter with the Art Institute Ghost, but not his last. He tells of another night when he and five friends were partying in the tower. Their laughter came to a sudden halt at the sound of footsteps approaching. "The steps came up, up, up," he says. "Just as they reached the landing, one of us yanked the door open and yelled 'surprise!' We were the ones who were surprised—there was no one there. The steps continued on, going all the way to the top of the tower."

Wally Hedrick, former long-time faculty member, said his most frightening brush with the ghost occurred one night when he was working after midnight. Suddenly, he heard all the tools go on downstairs in the sculpture studio. Hurrying down to investigate, he found no one.

Working as evening registrar during those days artist Hayward King, like many others, also began to believe in the ghost. He remembers closing the school at 10 p.m. "There was no master switch then, so we would walk all around the Institute, turning off lights as we went. Just before going out we'd turn and look back. Often we'd find that one or two lights were on again in the empty building. Of course you could say that we'd missed those lights or there was a short in the electricity. You could say a lot of things..."

Once King and Hedrick closed the office together after all the lights had presumably been turned off. As they shut the front door, every light in the building turned on simultaneously.

Morehouse, Hedrick and King believed their ghost to be mischievous but essentially benevolent. The unexplained manifestations that livened their evenings became less and less frequent until the ghost was almost forgotten.

Then in 1968 it returned. This time its appearance was decidedly disturbing.

As a 1.7 million dollar enlargement program began, attention was once more focused on the tower, which was being renovated as a storage facility for the Institute's Art Bank Collection. It seems that a slumbering ghost was awakened.

Several students on the night maintenance shift were convinced that the ghost was not only an evil influence on their own lives but was holding up the construction project. Three of the night crew blamed the spirit for personal disasters that included a serious motorcycle accident, an attack of polio and a tragic family situation.

Another told of studying late at night in the library with his wife. "We heard the sound of chairs being broken behind us, but no one was there," he said. The building program was delayed for many months by a series of costly mistakes and near-fatal accidents.

In response to an outbreak of incidents, a group of psychics gathered for a séance in the Institute tower. With them were several observers, myself included. Frustration was the emotion picked up by all the mediums. "So many artists with such grand designs that never got anywhere...so many trying to put their ideas on canvas...many projects uncompleted."

San Jose medium Amy Chandler told of seeing a "lost graveyard," a fact later verified by the Institute historian. A cemetery adjacent to the Institute had been obliterated by early 20th Century construction.

A series of pictures taken that evening by Nick Nocerino revealed the tower room not as it was but as it had been—with a door and windows that no longer exist. Others taken by Chuck Pelton showed a strange displacement of people within the room—a kind of musical chairs effect. Séance participants were photographed in motion, some fading in and out entirely. In reality none of us moved from our chairs during the two-hour session.

What that means, only the ghost can explain.

The San Francisco Art Institute is located at 800 Chestnut Street (at Jones).

Reprinted from Haunted Houses of California *(1990) by Antoinette May, with the kind permission of Wide World Publishing/Tetra.*

**The Bell Tower. Photograph by Philip Kaake.
Courtesy the San Francisco Art Institute.**

The Montandon Townhouse

by Antoinette May

"I lay a curse upon you and upon this house; I do not forget and I do not forgive; remember that!"

Can evil, angry words carry a power of their own? Is fact truly stranger than fiction?

Pat Montandon certainly has reason to think so. After reading her book, *The Intruders,* one finds it difficult to disagree.

During the 1960s the dazzling blond achieved recognition in San Francisco as hostess of a popular TV show. She gained national fame when listed by *Esquire Magazine* as one of the top hostesses in the country. The image, sustained by many flashbulbs and much newsprint, was "glamorous jet set queen." Here was a woman who seemingly had everything.

Unfortunately "everything" included a haunted house on Lombard Street.

It all began with a party, one more gala star-studded event in a glittering chain. This gathering—in keeping with the astrological renaissance of the late sixties—had a zodiac theme. An added attraction was a Tarot card reader.

The warm, festive mood turned to chill when the seer, piqued by an imagined slight, suddenly turned on Pat and snarled, "I lay a curse upon you..."

The words returned to haunt her in the years that followed, fearful years that found the golden butterfly ensnared in a web of dark malevolence. Her house was repeatedly vandalized and fire-ravaged. Her car was smashed several times, her career disrupted, her

reputation threatened by ugly accusations, her
romances blighted.

Locked windows within the house opened of their own
accord. A chill defied the normally functioning heating
system and totally destroyed the warm ambience of the
luxury townhouse. Two close friends who shared the
house committed suicide. Repeated threats on Pat's own
life forced her to hire round-the-clock guards but they
could not protect her from the evil atmosphere that
seemed to pervade her very being.

"I don't believe that the Tarot reader caused these
things," she has emphasized. "But possibly something in
that ugly incident triggered evil forces already hovering
about me or about the house itself—once the scene of
public hangings.

"Such thoughts would have been inconceivable to me
a few years ago," she admits, "but today it would be
impossible *not* to believe."

Certainly the most tragic of the circumstances
surrounding Pat's residence on crooked Lombard Street
was the death of her closest friend and secretary in one
of the most mysterious fires ever investigated by San
Francisco Fire Department.

On June 20, 1969 a blaze unaccountably started in
the master bedroom where Mary Louise Ward—who was
discovered dead in bed after the fire—had been sleeping
in Pat's absence. Firemen had difficulty entering the
house for the front door was chained and barred from
the inside. The possibility that Mary Louise had accidentally started the fire while smoking in bed was ruled out.
She didn't smoke. That a guest might have been responsible also seemed unlikely, for the bedroom door was
also *locked from the inside.*

Though an autopsy revealed that the victim was dead
before the fire, the actual cause of her death was *not*
determined. There was no evidence of heart failure,

sedation or drunkenness. Mary Louise's internal organs were in good condition and she had not suffocated. The investigation was finally dropped, the cause of death remaining a mystery.

Pat moved from the besieged townhouse but continued to be haunted by the experience. Concerned for the safety of the new tenants, she enlisted the aid of two mediums, Gerri Patton and Nick Nocerino. At her request, the two psychic investigators visited the house.

Though Nocerino knew nothing of its history, he was able to pick up psychically not only Pat's traumatic experiences, but also those of previous tenants unknown to her. His impressions were specific, including names and details. Research on Pat's part revealed that the former residents had indeed been involved in a series of tragic events that resulted in divorce, great personal loss and/or suicide.

The strangest incident connected with the investigation involved photographs taken by Nocerino inside the house. These revealed weird light configurations, despite the *absence* of artificial lights (light bulbs, flash bulbs, chandeliers or cut glass, etc.) with their capacity for reflection. Some prints clearly show a woman bending over a drawer with one hand raised as though in surprise at some discovery. The image was not on the negative and there was no one in the room at the time except Nocerino who was taking the pictures.

In an effort to verify the authenticity of the prints, Montandon arranged to have the negatives printed again under laboratory conditions with five independent witnesses present. The freshness of the chemicals was determined, negatives were brushed with a static-free brush, the time of exposure was recorded and every step of the development process observed by all. Shapes appeared on the prints that were not on the negative and several looked as though light was coming from some source. The same ghostly face and figure of a woman was again clearly visible although no such person had been seen or intentionally photographed in the house. Since the whole roll had been shot there, there seemed no possibility of a double exposure.

Hoping to avert more tragedy, Nocerino performed an exorcism on the house. "It was difficult to bring myself to give validity to such an act," Montandon admitted to me, "and yet, I no longer feel uneasy about the place. Everything now appears to be stable and normal."

One can only hope.

The house, a private residence, is located on San Francisco's "crooked Lombard Street."

Reprinted from Haunted Houses of California *(1990) by Antoinette May, with the kind permission of Wide World Publishing/Tetra.*

Murder So Foul

by Barbara Smith

The year was 1890. The ship, a Norwegian craft named the *Squando,* was docked at San Francisco when her captain discovered that his wife had been unfaithful to him. Worse, the woman's lover was the ship's first mate. Although the names of those involved in the tragic ocean-going triangle have been lost to time, their actions have left a permanent legacy.

Once she realized that her unfaithful act had been found out, the captain's wife immediately rediscovered her long-lost respect for her wedding vows—and together the devious married couple plotted the indiscreet sailor's murder. She coaxed the unsuspecting first mate into drinking far more than was good for him. As soon as he was too intoxicated to defend himself, the woman held her former lover still while her husband swung an ax across his neck. Seconds later they threw his body—and then his head—overboard.

The following morning, the murderers were in for an unpleasant surprise; the headless corpse had surfaced and was floating in plain sight through the waters of San Francisco Bay. The couple fled the ship in terror. This left the *Squando* without either a captain or a first mate. Although no record exists of the captain and his wife ever being brought to justice for their terrible deed, we do know that the company that owned the *Squando* kept the vessel in service. At least tried to.

The next three captains hired by the shipping company were all killed while on board the *Squando*. The ship developed a well-deserved reputation for being either jinxed or haunted—or both. In 1893, while the *Squando* was docked in Eastern Canada, the entire crew abandoned the ship. Word spread throughout the shipping community, and the ill-fated vessel's owner soon found that no sailor in the world would sign on for duty aboard the cursed vessel. The owners had little choice but to leave her docked where she was.

To prevent looting, the company hired local men to guard the ship. Within a few shifts, each one of a succession of guards had deserted the craft. Not one of them ever worked a moment beyond the time they saw the bloody, headless apparition lurking in the dark hallway by the captain's quarters.

The owners may not have believed the wild tales they were hearing about their ship, but they did know that a commercial craft that could be neither manned nor guarded served no purpose whatsoever. No doubt thinking they were putting an expensive but necessary end to the horror of the *Squando,* the Norwegian company ordered her torn apart and sold for salvage.

Apparently their solution was not an entirely successful one; recently, witnesses standing on San Francisco's Sky Deck Observatory at Embarcadero Center described a ship they had seen sailing out from a fog bank—a ship meeting the exact description of the long-destroyed *Squando.* Her demolition had seemingly only changed her from a ship of the physical world to a phantom ship from another dimension.

This story and the f   g one are reprinted from Ghost Stories of California *(2   y Barbara Smith, with the kind permission of the author and Lone Pine Publishing.*

Ghostly Lifesaver

by Barbara Smith

Despite its often pleasant climate, rolling hills and
spectacular bay views, San Francisco is not a good place
to be down on your luck. Unfortunately, that is exactly
the situation in which two young men, Eric and Peter,
found themselves at some point during the mid-1950s.
By the time they met up with the captain of a tramp
steamer, the two men were broke, hungry and, in a
word, desperate—desperate enough to accept the captain's offer of work that was described to them as being
"legal but dangerous."

Eric and Peter were aboard the steamer and a good
five days sail from San Francisco when, in the middle of
the night, a vicious fire broke out aboard. Angry-looking
flames soon engulfed the entire vessel, leaving the crew
no alternative but to don lifejackets and plunge into the
sea. By the time the first thin light of dawn crested the
horizon, the ship was gone. Eric and Peter were both
still alive, but just barely. The two men were totally
exhausted, too tired to go anything but simply float and
wait for death to claim them as she had claimed the
crewmates whose bodies bobbed lifelessly around them
in the water.

The two were so resigned to the inevitability of their
fate that, when Peter first saw an apparent mirage, he
was sure it was a near-death hallucination. *No one*
could be out rowing a small craft in the middle of the
Pacific Ocean. And yet, that is precisely what he thought
he saw. Surely, Peter mused, it was his fast-approaching
death from dehydration that caused the image to appear
in his mind's eye. He was confused, therefore, when he
saw Eric staring intently in the same direction—

apparently at the same image which Peter had been certain was merely a figment of his own demented imagination.

Neither Eric nor Peter could believe their ears when, moments later, the man in the tiny craft began to speak to them. The man explained that he was the sole survivor of a ship that had gone down in the area. Peter refused to waste what little energy he had left by trying to communicate with an illusion, but Eric struggled to ask the man if he had any food or drink that he would be willing to share. As if in reply, the strange man at the oars reached into the water and pulled out a good-sized fish, which he immediately proceeded to break in half. As he handed one half to Eric and the other to Peter, he told them, "Drink the water from its innards and then chew on its flesh for sustenance."

The young men did as they were instructed. The nourishment restored their strength sufficiently to climb into the rowboat with the man. Peter and Eric tried to thank their rescuer, but he seemed to have become disoriented and kept berating himself for having been a fool.

The motley trio spent the entire day crowded into the small craft and floating in the middle of the Pacific Ocean. By dusk they were able to row toward a deserted island, where they spent the night.

When the first light of dawn woke the young men the next morning, they were surprised to see that their Good Samaritan was preparing to leave in his little boat. Before he rowed off, however, he asked the stranded young men if they would do a favor for him. Without consulting one another, both Eric arid Peter eagerly agreed to help the kind man who had saved their lives.

"I'm going to tell you my wife's address, and also the number for a safety deposit box in San Francisco," he explained. "The key for the box is in the shed behind my

wife's house. I want my wife to have everything that is in
that box."

"But, what if we're not rescued?" Eric asked.

"You will be," the man assured the pair. As he rowed
away from Eric and Peter he called out, "You'll be safely
back in San Francisco in just a few days."

With their companion gone both men's hearts sank.
Eric and Peter lay on the shore of a tiny island that was
not much more than an outcropping of rock. Once again
the young men were sure that they would soon be dead.
Just when their spirits were at lowest ebb, fate seemed
to deal them an even more crushing blow. An airplane
flew low overhead, tantalizing them with the realization
that, while they had little chance of being rescued, they
were apparently not many miles from civilization. As the
two watched in amazement, the plane's cargo hold
opened up and a parcel was tossed out.

Eric reached the package first.

"Look!" he cried, tearing open the lifesaving pack of
supplies. Inside was something even more important
than the much needed food and water—a three-word
message reading, "Ship On Way." Early the next morning, the two young men who'd given themselves up for
dead twice in the space of just a few days watched in
wide-eyed wonder as a ship steamed toward them.

Once they were safely on board the Coast Guard res-
cue vessel, both Eric and Peter asked how they had
come to be found. While he was giving them blankets
and hot drinks, a sailor explained that a man in a rowboat had advised the Coast Guard of the stranded men's
position. Although they were thoroughly confused by all
that had happened, Peter and Eric were also extremely
relieved, so they settled in to enjoy the sail back to port.

When they'd recovered sufficiently from their grueling
experience, Eric and Peter set about making good on
their promise to the man in the rowboat. As soon as

they had located the correct address, they went to see their rescuer's wife. The woman greeted the young men with mild amusement but did allow that, yes, there was a shed in her backyard and, yes, they were more than free to inspect it if doing so would make them happy.

Moments later, she was astonished to see that the two strangers were handing her a key and delivering a message: "Your husband said that this key will fit a safety deposit box at your bank." They then repeated the box number that the man in the rowboat had given them.

The woman became nearly hysterical at the news. She told Eric and Peter that their information could not possibly be correct—her husband had been dead for eight years. He had died after falling overboard from the deck of a cargo ship sailing out of San Francisco, and his body had never been recovered. All three now realized that the young sailors had been rescued by a ghost—a ghost who then used the lads as messengers to get specific information to his widow. The sailor's wife later opened the safety deposit box and found it full of cash.

Checks into marine accidents off the coast of San Francisco during 1948 bear out this fantastic story. Records show that, during a vicious storm, the captain of a large sailing vessel ordered his crew to come on deck. Unfortunately, one of those sailors—a man matching the description of the mysterious apparition who'd rescued Eric and Peter—was drunk. In his confused state, the man failed to understand that a hurricane was approaching. He climbed into a small rowboat and lowered it into the turbulent ocean. Perhaps the poor man was somehow hoping to flee from the danger.

Neither the tiny, inadequate craft nor the drunken sailor manning its oars was ever seen alive again.

Victorian-Era Fiction

The Victorian Era—the last half of the 19th century—was a fertile period for fiction, both novels and short stories. And ghosts and the world of the supernatural were popular topics. San Francisco had numerous good writers and many of them used the City as a backdrop for their stories.

Most of the stories in this section are reprinted from *The Argonaut,* a weekly newspaper and literary journal that began publication in 1877. It was noted for its fine prose and poetry and featured such leading writers as Mark Twain, Bret Harte, and Ina Coolbrith. Although *The Argonaut* was published continuously until 1958, its heyday was its first two decades of existence when founder and editor Frank Pixley was in charge.

The story with the provocative title "Are the Dead Dead?" was written by Emma Frances Dawson (1851–1926), who was a protégé of Ambrose Bierce. A part-time writer and an award-winning poet, she supported herself by giving music lessons and teaching school. Described as modest and shy, in later years she became a recluse and died in poverty in Palo Alto.

She was well known in her time as a contributor to *The Argonaut* and other periodicals but is virtually forgotten today. "Are the Dead Dead?" wraps a ghost story around one of unrequited love.

"The Herald of Fate" by Charles Dwight Willard (1861–1914), with its ironic twist at the end, prefigures by about three generations the types of stories found in Alfred Hitchcock's classic TV series of the 1950s and

1960s, and the old Dell paperback mysteries that came out under Hitchcock's name.

Although the story takes place in San Francisco, Willard lived most of his working life in Los Angeles. A native of Chicago, he moved to California for his health after graduating from the University of Michigan in 1883. After roaming the state, and visiting San Francisco, he settled in Los Angeles where he worked alternately as a journalist for various newspapers and as a businessman. In the latter capacity he served as secretary of the Los Angeles Chamber of Commerce for six years in the 1890s. He contributed freelance articles to *The Argonaut* and other periodicals in his spare time.

Prolific author and journalist Ambrose Bierce (1842–c.1914), known as "Bitter Bierce" for his acerbic newspaper pieces, wrote many short stories, nearly all of which had touches of the macabre. "Beyond the Wall" provides a representative example. Bierce disappeared in Mexico in late 1913, during the Mexican revolution, and was never heard from again.

"A Mirage of Murder" by Howard Markle Hoke (b.1857?) tells a ghostly tale of murder. Hoke seems to have written a few stories for non-San Francisco periodicals, but this one appears to be the only story he had published in *The Argonaut,* which is where "Mirage" first saw print, in 1895. Hoke is not listed in any directories of California authors, and thus biographical information on him is scant.

"Who Believes in Ghosts!" may be the one pure ghost/haunted house story Jack London (1876–1916) ever wrote, which is surprising considering his background. His father, who abandoned him before he was born, was an itinerant astrologer, and his mother was a part-time spiritualist. This story is one of London's earliest; he wrote it while a senior in high school. He was not yet at the peak of his powers, and the story reveals a bit of youthful showing off as London drops references into the narrative to *Trilby,* a recently published novel, and to Emile Gaboriau, a French mystery writer and creator of detective Inspector Lecoq.

"Over an Absinthe Bottle," although not a ghost story in the traditional sense, concludes with a ghostly out-of-body experience. It's author, William C. Morrow (1854–1923), was a native of Alabama who started his writing career in the Bay Area as a journalist for newspapers in San Francisco and San Jose. He wrote a few novels, but is best known for his finely crafted short stories, which appeared in *The Argonaut,* the *Californian,* and the *San Francisco Examiner.* In later years Morrow taught fiction writing.

"Are The Dead Dead?" (Abridged)

by Emma Frances Dawson

"You ought to join the Ghost Club."

"What do you mean?" I asked. "I had not heard of one."

"Well, it is kept quiet," my caller said; "but it is a small club whose members go to houses said to be haunted, to see what truth there may be in the tales. You know that one out on Valencia Street, near Fifteenth? They have spent some time there; and in the large house here in town, on Sutter Street, which was vacant so long, and at last taken, with its fine grounds, for a beer-garden."

"What happened?" I asked. "Was anyone frightened into a fit?"

"No," said he, "they have seen nothing yet. But if you watch to-morrow night, you will see them marching up here to the house over the way."

I began to be interested, "That house!" I said; "I did not know anything was the matter with it. But I know it has been long to let." I did not tell him what a part of my reveries it had been—not only for its picturesque look, but also because of the music I had once heard from its windows.

"It is not easy to let," he went on, "because the first owner poisoned himself there. Why don't you join the club? You are fanciful enough. I can give you letters to the chief members."

"I might—for fun," I said; "I have no faith."

"Neither have they: they call it a quest for truth."

I let him write the letters—two to women, one to a man—three out of the seven who formed the club.

The last thing that night I paused by my window to look
over at the house—square, high, dark, outlined against
the stars, far above the street, which was cut through
the hill at some date since the building of the house,
which stands near the head of about a hundred zigzag
steps, with landings here and there at the turns, the
first flight boarded from the street, and looking like a
switch-tender's hut on a railroad.[1]

Behind an uncared-for garden of dusty evergreens,
and half-hidden in yellow and white jasmine, the lonely
house, with its closed windows, made me think of a
giant with shut eyes lying in a garden under a spell. Did
it ever dream? Sometimes I half believed in flitting lights
and changeful shadows behind one shutterless window
up-stairs, but thought it must be the reflection of the
head-light of a passing street car dummy.[2]

That house had long been like a conscious comrade
in my day-dreams. It was linked in my mind with an
offer of marriage I once had from one for whom I cared
very little, but whom circumstances nearly brought me
to accept. But through the open windows came such a
strain of warning music that, creatures of chance
impulses that we are, swayed by a look or a tone, my
mind changed in spite of me. I was lifted out of my
usual self, and had strength to do right. I never knew
anything of the unseen singer, but his love for his art as
shown by daily study, which I heard. That "sound which

---

1. It was common for city streets in the 19th century to be graded
   and lowered after houses had been built. Many examples still
   exist today, with houses high above their streets, accessible
   only by climbing multiple stairs to reach the front door.
2. Early cable car lines had two attached vehicles, the lead car of
   which was the "dummy." It contained the grip and other levers
   used in operating the line. It towed a passenger car behind it.

was a soul" surely saved me from making my life a mere, hard, rude outline, from losing all the picturesque effects of light and shade which romance, hope, and feeling give. I could not help wishing to join the Ghost Club, though thought our pains would be vain. I felt a strange interest in the plan. It made me restless that night. While dressing in the morning I looked up again at the lonesome-looking house, and, nodding gaily toward it, cried: *"You* have haunted *me!"*

No one could have felt lighter-hearted and more free from dread than I as during the day I presented my letters, and gained consent to my joining the club "for that one house." Heaven knows I have now no wish to thus visit another!

When the club gathered that night at the doorway to the steps over the way, I joined them. A queer group. A believer, a doubter, an inquirer, a strict church member, and others who came, as I did, for pastime. Some were late, and had not yet come when we wound up the long stairs, and waited at the door for some one who was to bring the key.

As we went into the house, I found in the man who had the key an old neighbor.

"Why, Mr. H——!" I cried.

He started nervously, and looked around in great surprise. "Miss W——!" said he, "are *you* here?—with those asking eyes of yours?"

"Oh, I don't believe in it," I laughed; " I am only curious, like the rest."

Not so much then as since, I have thought of his strange look at me, and the shrug of his shoulders, which seemed to lift me off his mind, for he paid no more heed to me that night.

The others glanced here and there through the open doors, with an eager air, in marked contrast with Mr.

H——'s studied unconcern. They noticed his manner, and spoke of it.

"I never look about me in *this* house," he said, gravely, "or in any of these old places," he added, and hurried off.

As we stood in the hall, another member made us a speech about being in a fit state, and urged that we should be placed in rooms by ourselves, or no more than two together. Though, after some wrangling, we were allowed a light in each room, we were to sit idle and not speak. I was left in a small room, with a window on the street. The others went where he told them. The silence which soon reigned made it seem as if there was no one in the house. Fearless as I had always boasted of being, a strange dread at last settled on me. I could not lose that feeling as of some one just at the door, which we know in vacant furnished houses. I tried to forget why we came. I counted, each way, the figures in carpet and curtains. I noticed all in the room, the common and uncommon, from chairs, table, and sofa to a veiled picture and an old-fashioned secretary, whose torn green silk behind the glass doors showed some stray leaves of manuscript.

I wondered in which room the old owner took poison. Supposing it to be true, as some have thought, that suicide chains the spirit to earth, why should we know it? What right had we to pry into the unknown? I shrank from the test, and was seized with nervous trembling. Even my dog, which I had brought along, grew restless, and ran home just as, much to my relief, a late-comer entered the house.

He came in the room, where I was—a shy, quiet young man, who went toward the window, but suddenly seeing me, started, stared, and dropped into a seat. It struck me some way that he was in awe of me. I was half amused to think he might be taking a stranger for a ghost.

Long we sat amid the shadows, silent and strange, as if both by some spell called up from the shades by the club. The oil lamp burned dimly. I faintly saw my companion's glowing eyes, and fine profile like that on antique vase or coin, and the small spray of the breath-of-heaven's snowflake flowers that with a blood-red pink he wore as a button hole bouquet.

I could not keep my eyes off this man. Dazed, I looked at him. Where had I known him? I seemed flooded by a tidal wave of memories—of what?—bits of dreams?—sleeping or waking ones? Was it a tide of inherited memories surging through my veins with the hot blood of some ancestress who had, like me now, loved at first sight one like him, this man of graceful movement and head like an antique bust? Who could tell? I gazed at him, mad with vague, keen longing and remembrance, excited as with wine by the new and piquant charm of feeling the overwhelming power of his presence, yet seeing him wholly unaware of it, and even shy. I was under a spell subtle as the scent of the blossoms that nestled, where I longed to lay my head, upon his breast.

When the hours of our fruitless waiting had passed, and we all stumbled down the winding, grass-grown steps, from star-light through shadow into the gas-lit street, I was dizzy with the intoxication of his glances, and lay awake the rest of the night. Who was he? One of this crazy club. I wanted nothing to do with them. I resolved not to join them again. But just as I had waked all night I dreamed all day.

As the day wore on, I could not keep from going up there to look about in the light. The key had been left with me. I took it, but hardly meant to use it. I thought I would walk in the garden. The still, old place had an odd charm for me. It was so solitary, that, though the

sunshine was over all, and an army of wallflowers
formed their torch-lit ranks round the door, there
seemed to be no relief from a weight of loneliness. It
seemed almost remote enough for Death to overlook.
Was it haunted? The house looked at me with its pleasant windows, and lured me to go in. The sense of intru-
sion was too strong for me to go all over it. I went into
the room where I sat the night before. I had not paused
to mark the dusty gloom, or to feel nervous, when I happened to glance through the glass of the secretary, I
bent to admire the writing thrust behind the worn green
silk. I saw my own Christian name. I opened the doors.
Fragments which had lain there by chance so long,
plainly worthless, at the mercy of the next tenant, whoever it might be. I took them by right of my name of
Rose. They were leaves torn from a note-book, mostly
the record of a singer's daily practice: so many minutes
to these exercises, or to those, or to songs, and so much
time to French and Italian. But here and there came
these entries:

This evening I saw her sitting in her window, looking
lonely and sad, for her drooping head reminded me of a
heavy-hearted flower. Could I be but her sheltering and
supporting leaf! But I am like the ground at the feet of
my Rose—no more able to come near her sweet lips, or
touch her dainty hand! Soon her curtains were drawn.
Into the moonlit space between our houses, from the
depths of my heart, I sang Fesca's impassioned "Maiden
at the Window."

        *   *   *   *   *   *   *

How hard is my fate! My mind is like a phantom bat-
tle-field, with this conflict carried on in silence—an
awful, noiseless war, as of shadows; but to me, what

dread realities! Sometimes I think I *must* break my bond
with my cousin. What a cursed fool I was to bargain
away my freedom for the sake of her money, for study
here and in Europe. But love to me was only a name.
When I made that contract I had not seen Rose.

      *   *   *   *   *   *   *

To see Rose sitting here before me, to hear her say, "I
love you!" would be enough to come back from another
world. But what we miss here must be gone forever.

      *   *   *   *   *   *   *

This was all of the journal. I was amazed at these bits
of shattered romance, for the writer had long been
known abroad, and I had read of his being made
court-singer for life in a far-off country. It was like too
late looking down some charming road one might have
taken. I sighed. Was my sigh echoed, or was it the
sound of the swaying boughs of the old gum-trees? I
could not say. I ran home to think it over. I was still lost
in wonder over it when, in spite of my resolves, I joined
the club that night.

We were placed as before. I thought of the odd folks
now in these rooms, queer as the thoughts that lurk in
the cells of a madman's brain. I waited, like them, but
not for the same reason. I was anxious for *his* coming,
though I felt faint and ready to run home to shun meeting his eyes. What if he did not come? At the thought, a
weight on my spirits changed the look of the room, as a
cloud dulls the sunny landscape. With a thrill, a shiver
of delight, I heard him enter.

As he stood for a moment looking at me over the lamp
on the table, the faint radiance making his statuesque
beauty glow out of the dimness as if conjured by a spell,

the scent of the breath-of-heaven and clove-pink in his button hole might have been that of spices burned for an incantation. What was it I saw in those fine eyes? Neither scorn nor pity; they were kind, but full of an overwhelming surprise.

"Again!" he murmured; then kept the club rule of silence.

I was confused. I could scarcely breathe. My head whirled. I reeled to a chair. The flickering rays of the lamp danced about him, like restless thoughts, while we waited. Waited? I forgot the club, the house, that I was in the city, in the world. I knew only that the man I loved sat before me.

After even the little I had known of the club disputes, I was not surprised to see the pale young man shun the others when we all left. As we went out into the windy night, the well-known street and view seemed new. I felt as if I had left the real world behind; that, truly, one "lived" only in "raptures and desolations." San Francisco, the club, were vague phantoms, dreams within dreams. I roused to myself at my own gate, with Mr. H——'s voice in my ear:

"Are these all?" he asked, looking after the members going down the street. And watching, with a pang of regret, their vanishing forms, I forgot to answer.

Then I cried: "Mr. H——, it has just come back to me how you urged my folks not to take that very house a year or two ago. Why did you do so?"

"I don't want to see anyone live in it," he answered. "My friend K——, the rare tenor, used to be there. Poor fellow! He was to have married a cousin, whose money helped him to study music; but I have always thought that his heart was elsewhere. She held him in a thrall, which wore upon him; and the voice, most frail of all instruments, is hurt by worry. His was, and at last left him. This shock, and disappointment, killed him."

"Oh, I am so sorry!" I cried. "I never saw him, but I shall not forget his voice. In 'Robin Adair' it was like the flute of the twilight wind."

"Yes," said Mr. H——. "As I stood by his grave, I thought of what Antipater said over the tomb of Orpheus: 'Here lies a poet; here lies a soul that sang; here lies the sound of the wind.' He did not want to die though he would say to me, '*Then* I shall be free!' His cousin, a spiteful woman, seemed to hate to have him escape her control, though he did that whenever he sang. His voice raised a magic wall around him—we could only listen afar. After his death, she said to me, 'He has got away from me now—but *wait till I die!*' with a motion that was a threat. She would not return here, and has been trying to have the house sold."

"But why did you not want us to move there?" I asked.

"He once said to me," Mr.H—— went on: "If when I dream, I can see the old house, go over it, see *her* in the window across the way, may it not be that such plea-sure, felt by me now through none of the nerves of sense, will be known to my spirit after I die? Perhaps unheard, unseen, the two worlds blend, and we shall move along our old paths, with rare visions of the living, who will seem unreal and awful to us. I wonder if my soul could then affect one I loved, or must I be a flitting specter with no power. We shall see."

"Then you believe?" I began.

"I have no belief," he said, quickly. "It seems to me nothing is too strange to happen."

No, I thought, after he left me, I should wonder at nothing after feeling this sudden deep interest in two strangers, such regret for the singer, and such absorb-ing passion for my companion of the last two evenings. Why had I not asked Mr. H—— who he was?

The next night I meant should be my last with the club, shrunk this time to just three others and myself.

The small room where I sat had at once a charm and a sadness for me. I was filled with the vain desire to have known its old tenant. I wondered about the end of such strong passions as his. Can they cease here? Are they merely to brighten our path like vivid colors in flowers and sky? In fancy I heard again the lovely tenor airs from "Lucia," "Faust" and "Martha" which had of old rung through this window. I thought of his journal. But through it all ran the stronger undercurrent of longing for the coming of the pale young member of the club.

He entered and started at seeing me, and, pausing an instant, murmured: "Once more!" and sank into a chair which stood back to the door; and again I was spell-bound by his shy, but ardent gaze, by the scent of the same sweet flowers he wore.

With none of my suitors, thronging like bees about the honey of my wealth, had I ever felt this tumult of emotion. I was glad of the club-rule of silence. I could have thrown myself into his arms, but I could not speak.

Sitting there so long, so still, it seemed to my strained nerves that we were like ghosts, and only the pictures on the wall had life and emotion. The hall-clock groaned twelve times, but my watch lacked ten minutes of twelve. A cold draught rushed in as at the opening and closing of some of the doors. A nameless fear seized me. But a woman I had not yet seen with the club looked in at the open door, surprise, doubt, and scorn in her intent face.

A woman more to be feared than a ghost, I thought, as I marked her evil look. She paused in amaze at sight of us. Suddenly the dim light wholly failed. To be in the dark was to recall the errand here of the club. It could not be borne, even with others near me. After crossing what seemed an endless space, I reached the mantel, felt for a match, found one, and groped back to the center-table.

As I lighted the lamp I saw him watching me with questioning eyes, as if unmoved by the loss of the light or its return. I saw her looking in with a wicked smile. A jealous woman, I judged—all the more as she drew back before he could turn to find the cause of my changed looks. But he was curious enough to leave the room. Was she his wife? Was I bewitched by a man bound to another woman? Has each case its like? Was another man in this very house held in bonds? These questions perplexed me all night.

The next afternoon I went over to look for a favorite lace handkerchief, dropped in coming out with the club. I found it caught on a thistle near the top stair. It was Sunday, and the chimes of Saint Patrick's Church[3] came to me clear and sweet.

I looked at the old house, longed and yet did not like to go in. But I knew none of the club were likely to come until night, when they were to make their last visit, and as for ghosts, had we not tested it?

I pushed in through the dreary hall. I passed on into the small front room. It gave me the same feeling of sorrow and regret. It was like the return from a funeral.

How sorry I now felt that I had never known the people who used to live here. I had often thought, perhaps the friends we never meet might have been the dearest. I could not tear myself away. For the first time by daylight I looked from the window, which, to my surprise, had a

---

3. Constructed between 1870 and 1872, St. Patrick's Church still stands on Mission Street just east of Fourth Street (across from Yerba Buena Gardens). The church was partially destroyed by the 1906 earthquake but was rebuilt.

full view of my own room across the way. They must
have known more of me than I ever knew about them.

The house shook in the wind, as if stirred by unseen
hands, but in the room all was still as if in a picture.
There were the rusty nails and black moss in the
grass-grown garden and stairs, as at the "moated
grange," but no fly buzzed in the window, no mouse
squeaked in the wainscot, no bird chirped on the roof.
Nothing moved but the clock in the hall, and the shadow
of a gum-tree across the floor. My little dog and I sat still
as statues.

I looked out of the window, and saw the buildings of
the city far below stand out in the light of the sinking
sun, with sudden sharp lines, as long-forgotten things
startup in the mind of one dying. Why were my thoughts
all of death? Then a line of phantoms of silent tunes,
long since sung here, passed by my ears. I thought of
the surprise and dislike in that woman's face the night
before, and of what slight ground for jealousy she had,
when he and I sat in such silence—but recalling his
speaking eyes, my heart's quickened beating, and the
flushes I felt mount my cheeks, I knew she had good
cause.

I was vexed at myself, both for being here almost
against my will, and for a nervous fear which had come
over me when once inside the house. I would not yield
to it.

A long-drawn sigh, which sounded close by me, made
me look up. I was startled. My dog crouched at my feet
and barked. Had I left the front-door on the latch? I
rushed to see. Turning in the hall with the feeling of
being watched, I saw a woman's head peering round a
distant door. There was a familiar look about her.
Thinking it must be one of the club, I started toward
her, but she drew back and closed the door, which she
held against me.

Was she afraid of me? I laughed, a little nervously, wrenched it open—but no one was in sight. I called, no answer, but, glancing up, saw the same head hanging over the same banisters up-stairs, and part of her dress. I was struck with something so wicked in her look that my little Spitz ran cowering and whining to the street-door. But, thinking I ought to explain my presence there, I went up-stairs. To my surprise the woman, without waiting for me, passed down the long hall and turned a corner.

I hurried after, thinking I might have frightened her if she were a nervous member, and, in my haste, nearly fell through to the lower story, for at the turning yawned an opening where stairs had been taken down. My dress caught on a nail in the floor, and held me back just in time. As I freed my skirt I saw that from the hall-window, just beyond the pitfall, my house could be seen better than from down-stairs. A smothered chuckle, followed by a cry of rage, made me look down. The woman was watching me from below. There must be some other flight, I thought, yet found none, and went to the lower room, but she had hidden.

I turned to look for my dog. What was this fluffy mass by the hall-door? Not my gay little comrade? This poor creature in spasms! Some evil power was at work here. Even that cruel-faced woman would be welcome company. I called. No reply. I tried to open the outer door, but it seemed barred by the rusty, large lock, to which there was no key.

I strove to be brave. I went through the lower part. The back door was fast. I thought she must have fled that way. It was awful to be alone there. I saw nothing strange, but felt as if dogged, doors opening behind me as soon as I closed them. I tried to think it was caused by the jar of my steps and the uneven flooring, but I felt the Bible was right to forbid the calling of spirits. Had

not the Ghost Club brought all this horror upon me? It
made no odds that they had been searching to prove
there was no such thing. There was the ugly story of the
hanged man, whose body was dissected and his skull
ground to dust, yet in the night the bits were seen to
join, one by one, till the man was whole, and went out
of the door.

I went back to the front room. Trying to forget my
fears, I raised the gauze screen from the portrait over
the mantel. It was not unlike the face of the strange
woman! In my vexation toward her, I flung the veil
against it again. The next instant, my elbows were
fiercely gripped from behind. I was rushed swiftly toward
the window I had opened when I first came in. My heart
nearly stopped beating. Years of torture seemed crowded
in that one moment. I was to be thrown out, to fall from
that great height to the street! I shrieked in hopeless terror. I was suddenly cast on the floor, and when I could
look round, I saw that woman near the door, with her
hard face turned as if to listen.

Some one was on the steps. She glided out and was
upstairs, as the front door, forced by stronger hands
than mine, opened, and, to my deep relief and joy, the
pale young man came in. Braced by the relief of his
coming, then I could talk to him. He only nodded once
in a while, but his eyes again held mine. To my questions about the woman he shook his head, and seemed
surprised when I said: "She was here last night."

So she had gone when he went out. I did not wonder
she was jealous, as I stood there, hardly conscious of
anything but the charm of his presence, and the scent of
the bit of breath-of-heaven and blood-red pink he wore.
And he—he kept the club-rule of silence. But I thought I
knew what he was thinking. I had not slept since I had
last seen him. I passed the night watching, as I lay in
bed, the old house—looming dim and large against the

starry sky—or, half dozing, dreaming of flitting lights in the windows and echoing strains of music.

I had not slept for thinking of *him.* Those wonderful eyes! They seemed so near and dear a part of myself that I forgot we, were, as the world goes, strangers. Surely we had known each other for eternities.

"Where have you been all these years?" I said. "We must have known each other before, for I *love* you, and it is no new feeling. My life has been a dream, a nightmare—at last I am awake. Do not leave me again, for I could not bear it. Stay! Stay!"

"Oh, if it might only be!" he murmured.

He came nearer, bent over as if to kiss me, when a white hand was laid on his shoulder. He turned in amazement. *She* stood beside him.

"*You!*" he groaned, with a gesture of despair, and reeled back. He grew, if possible, more bloodless than ever. I could see him tremble. Dismay and dread in his face, and a hunted look came in his eyes.

With a look of triumph at me, she beckoned him. Making a motion toward me, as of mingled farewell and warning, he slowly went after her, though often turning to look back. I followed. They passed along the hall, where my dog lay dead, out of the front door and slowly down the long steps. At each landing he stopped and gazed back, then followed her into the dusk through which the members of the club were toiling up. Among them Mr. H——, with a lighted lantern. They paid no heed to the figures going down, and were surprised at my wild agitation.

"Look! Look!" I cried to Mr. H——.

"Why! Your eyes have been answered!" he muttered, staring at me.

"What is it?" "Where?" "When?" "What happened?" "What's the matter, H——?" urged the club.

"Let us get away from this house!" he cried, looking uneasily behind him, and signing to one of the members to lock the door. His hand trembled so, the lantern shook, as he said:

"I came over, in case any of you were here, to warn you, I have just heard Miss Edith L——, who lived here, died in Paris last night."

"Last night—at ten minutes of twelve o'clock?" I gasped, suddenly faint.

"Well—," he thought a moment, "yes—ten minutes past nine there, would just make it—how did you know of it?"

"Tall; light eyes; a set, stern face—not without malice?" I stammered.

"I thought you never saw her?" he said.

"Tall, dark, with a face like an antique bust, divine eyes?" I went on.

"Then you *had* seen him," said he. Struck by a sudden thought, he added: "Do you mean—can it be that you—how—where?"

I caught his arm. "See there!" I cried, pointing where the two forms—one; looking up over his shoulder—had passed on the lowest landing, but now moved on. Could it be that my touch made him see as I did?

"My God!" he cried, his nerveless hand dropping the lantern. "Then I was too late!"

I sank, limp and helpless, on the top stair. The glare of the lantern on the club's eager faces round me with their various looks of wonder, doubt, content, fear, and pity; the jeering sound of the fog-horn; the shock of such an end to my romance; a keen sense of life's "raptures and desolations'—all made me hysterical, as I burst forth:

"You—you think——?"

"I *know*," he answered, with awe-struck face, white to the very lips, that could scarcely say the words, "*you have seen the ghosts!*"

Reprinted from The Argonaut, *October 2 and 9, 1880.*

The Herald Of Fate

by Charles Dwight Willard

On a certain winter morning, a few years since, Mr.
Clark Rogers, who was the "Co." in the firm of Harkness,
Lyon & Co., in Sansome Street, appeared at the office
with a very unusual expression on his face. Harkness,
who was an affable, kindly man, noticed it, and asked
whether he was not feeling very much out of sorts that
morning. It did not escape Lyon, the practical managing
head of the firm, who ventured the remark that Rogers
evidently had something on his mind. The book-keepers,
who were accustomed to work under Mr. Rogers's direction, commented upon it at noon to one another, and
decided that something very queer must have happened
to affect him so deeply.

The something very queer which had upset the
matter-of-fact intellect of Clark Rogers, and had brought
the strained, bewildered look upon his face, was a letter
which the postman had delivered at his bachelor
apartments that morning. With the reading of that letter
a complete revolution had taken place in his mind. For
the first time in his life of forty-five years he was brought
face to face with something for which he could find no
conceivable explanation. Heretofore no problem had ever
presented itself to which his plain common sense was
not equal. Being now suddenly thrown from the regular
orbit which he was accustomed to traverse, the result
was something very like a panic.

The strange thing concerning this letter, which had
come regularly through the mail and bore the San
Francisco post-mark of the preceding day, was that it
came from a dead man. That Howard Russell was dead
there could be no doubt, for nearly twenty years before

Rogers himself had helped to carry his body to the
grave. They had been friends during their boyhood and
youth in a decaying New England town. On the other
hand, there seemed to be no possible doubt that this
letter was from Howard Russell. It was signed with his
name, was written unmistakably in his hand, and
contained references to things of which no one else
could know. After a strained effort to account for it all,
Mr. Rogers read and reread the letter, experiencing as
he did so a queer sensation of mental numbness. The
letter ran as follows:

My DEAR CLARK: You are doubtless astonished to receive
a letter in my hand-writing, and are vainly endeavoring to
account for it. For many years I have been wishing and striving to communicate with you, and at last I have found a
human medium through whom I can reach you; his hand
guided by mine writes you, and his body held by my soul can
speak the message I wish to send. I know that this is all out of
the range of your belief. Experience has never revealed to you
the possibility of the return of a human soul to the earth after
its departure from the body. I ask you to believe nothing, only
to listen. It is necessary that you should understand that it is
Howard Russell who writes this letter; therefore, I will remind
you of the pledge which I gave you when you talked with me
alone a few hours before my death, that I would return to
warn you if I foresaw any calamity to your life. I will remind
you, too, of the October afternoon when we strolled together
through the woods and talked of Mary, and solemnly agreed
to remain friends, whichever of us she might accept. Is this
sufficient? Can you imagine that anyone else should know of
these two occurrences?

It is for the sake of Mary that I wish to come to speak to
you, and because of the love which you once bore her you
are bound to listen. On the evening of the day when you read
this letter you will find yourself detained at the office by
unfinished work. There will come to you a man who will give

his name as Campion, and will offer to speak my words. You
shall listen to him, learn your destiny, and act upon the
advice which is tendered. Let not your disbelief in the possibility of this close your ears to the truth. Withhold judgment
for the present, but listen faithfully to my message.

THE SPIRIT OF HOWARD RUSSELL

Now, had anyone of Clark Rogers's friends, who were
wont to admire the cool, practical way in which he took
the affairs of life, related such an occurrence to him, he
would have been at no loss for an explanation "Some
enterprising swindler," he would have declared, "who
happened to have learned these facts about you, imi-
tates the dead man's hand-writing in the hope of getting
you to pay for further disclosures." Yet now the case was
of his own experience, this explanation was dismissed
almost without a hearing. For a time his thoughts continued to grope about blindly, striving to grasp anything
by which they could find their way back to light. There
seemed to be nothing within reach, and for once hopeless amazement ruled in his mind.

Mr. Clark Rogers had no relatives, and he was not in
the habit of making confidants of his few friends. His life
was essentially commonplace, methodical, and lonely.
He spent the days over the ledgers of Harkness, Lyon &
Co., and the evenings in his apartments or at the club.
He had come to the coast many years before, while still
a young man, and had slowly worked his way up from
poverty to affluence by the most strict attention to business. The property which he had thus acquired he proposed to leave to his sister's son, a young man of
considerable business promise, who lived in a city of the
middle West. Such a life was without perplexities of any
sort, and tended to make harder to bear anything
strange or unexpected which came to pass.

For these reasons, therefore, the face of Clark Rogers wore the troubled look which had attracted the notice of his partners and the clerks. The letter had advised him to suspend judgment until he should have further evidence, and in the effort to accomplish this, he found himself unable to keep his thoughts upon his work during the day. Had he been able to offer himself any explanation whatever, he might have dismissed the question from his mind, but in default of that it constantly returned to torment him. Presently a curious desire to see the conclusion of the affair took possession of him, and he began to wonder whether the alleged "medium" would put in an appearance. Under other circumstances it would have seemed to him preposterous that he should be brought to consider the idea of listening to an impostor of this stamp, but at present he was strangely eager for the interview. The prediction that he would be detained at the office in the evening proved true, for the reason that he found at the end of the day that he had accomplished but a small part of his accustomed labors.

At about nine o'clock that evening Mr. Rogers sat alone in his private office at the front end of the building on Sansome Street. To the rear, beyond the labyrinth of tables and showcases, were the glass compartments where a few book-keepers were still at work. Intent upon finishing the duties he had left undone during the day, Rogers was bending over the paper on his desk. The room was lighted dimly by an argand gas lamp. When at last he looked up, he discovered that he was no longer alone, but that a tall man, dressed in a shabby suit of black cloth, was standing near him. He had entered unnoticed, although both the street and office doors were closed. His arms were folded, and from under the brim of his black slouch hat a pair of great, deep-set eyes looked down upon the merchant.

"Good evening," said he, when Rogers looked up; "my name is Campion."

"How did you get in?" asked Rogers, in a startled tone.

"The doors open quietly, and you were much absorbed in your work," the man answered.

As it became more evident that his strange visitor was flesh and blood, and not some unearthly being, Mr. Rogers's calmness returned. He motioned the man to a seat opposite to himself in front of the desk, and, for a minute, looked intently at his face as the light fell on it from the gas-lamp. The medium's features were large and striking, and of a waxy paleness. After the short, searching gaze he had bestowed upon Mr. Rogers when he first entered, he did not again look at him, but allowed his great luminous eyes to stare blankly into space.

Presently, when Mr. Rogers felt his self-control sufficiently established to speak, he said: "Well, sir, what is your business with me?"

"I do not know," answered the man.

His method of speaking was quite as strange as his appearance. He spoke slowly, yet each sentence seemed to come at a breath. Although without emphasis or inflection, it was still not expressionless, for his voice was sonorous and the words clearly enunciated.

"You do not know! Then what did you come for?"

The man passed his hand wearily over his eyes.

"Because I was compelled to come. For several days I have been haunted by a spirit that would give me no rest until I had communicated his message to you. Yesterday I wrote you from him the letter, which I saw you receive, and which has been in your mind during all the day. You are so constituted as to be unable to believe what I say, so I need not trouble myself to assure you that I did not even know what that letter contained, just as I do not know now what I am destined to say to you, and can not retell it when the spirit is gone."

"See here," interrupted Rogers, sternly; "I am prepared to listen to what you have to communicate to me, for in some mysterious way you seem to be speaking for a dead man that I once knew. I will pay whatever fee is necessary, but do not try to make me believe what I know to be false."

The man shook his head.

"There will be no fee," said he.

"Very well, then," said the merchant; "I am prepared to listen to you."

There were a few minutes of silence. Rogers had pushed his chair back until he was out of the light of the lamp and several yards distant from his visitor. The latter sat motionless as a statue, his eyes fastened upon a spot in the wall. Presently his pale features began to twitch nervously, but he did not speak. His hands were clasped with an energy which denoted great mental strain. His breath came in long sighs, or in short, quick gasps.

All at once he turned his great eyes upon Rogers and began to speak, and at the first word the merchant started as if he had received a painful shock, for he heard again the sound of a voice stilled for many years in death.

"Clark, I need not tell you who it is that speaks to you, for you recognize me by my voice. Believe me, I am sorry to have given you this shock, but it was needed that you should know what is soon to come to pass. A calamity is about to happen to you, of which I must give you warning for the sake of the woman whom we once both loved. In the selfish life that you are leading it is many years since you even thought of Mary. You have not cared to learn whether she is happy or wretched, although at one time she was to have been your wife.

You knew that she was now a widow, but how she has maintained herself and her children you have not asked. In your narrow and severe way you have always blamed her for the separation which your neglect and coldness forced her to bring about. When she married, you dismissed her from your thoughts as having been unworthy of you. You are as selfish and as unfeeling now as you were when, by your superior strength of will, you compelled me to give her up.

"For years I have seen the woman I loved suffering from poverty and hardship, and have longed to help her. I knew that it was idle to communicate with you, for she is too proud to accept the slightest benefit from you while you are still alive. Events have at last taken a turn which puts it in your power to offer her assistance that she will not refuse.

"Clark Rogers, I come to warn you that the day of your death is at hand; it is not a month away, it is scarcely more than a week. The will which you had drawn up three years ago leaves the bulk of your property to your nephew. Within three days you will receive information through the newspapers of his betrayal of the trust imposed in him, and of his disgraceful flight. When you frame a new testament—and see that you do not delay in doing so—remember the woman whose life was rendered miserable by your selfish neglect. The money which you had intended to leave to your sister's unworthy son will go to repair the wrong which you wrought fifteen years ago. It will enable one of the noblest and truest women who ever lived to educate her children and spend the remainder of her life in peace and comfort, blessing your memory after you are dead."

The voice ceased, but the stranger sat with parted lips and dilated eyes, steadily gazing at the listener. From the first, Rogers had nerved himself to meet some sort of a shock, but the sound of the dead voice, the memory of a forgotten love, and the reference to his own death deprived him for a time of the self-control which was characteristic of him.

Gradually, however, he recovered himself, and determined that whatever internal misgivings might beset him he would put on a bold front to this man whom he believed to be an impostor. After a few moments of silence, he said, with apparent unconcern: "It is evident; whoever you are, that you know much about Howard Russell and myself, yet I am in no way affected by the pretended messages which you deliver. I do not believe in them at all. As to your effort to excite my fears by predicting my death, it will avail nothing. I am in too good health to allow my spirits to be touched by superstitious dread of such an event."

"As to your health, it is by no means what you believe it to be. On the day after to-morrow, as you sit down at your desk in the afternoon, you will experience a sudden fluttering of the heart, followed by a strained feeling in the arteries. This will be repeated at intervals, until you are compelled to consult a physician. I see you with him now. He is a short man, with bristling eye-brows and a gray mustache."

"My physician has a long black beard," said Rogers, grimly.

"The one you will consult has not. However, your death is not to be the result of illness, for I can see you a short time before the occurrence, and you are then a robust man, a little pale, but in good health."

"Since you can tell so much," said the merchant, "why do you not reveal it all to me, how and when my death is to take place?"

"I will tell you all that I can see," answered the clairvoyant. "You are before my eyes now, with death but a few moments away. You stand in a small room with white wooden walls. It resembles, in some degree, a state-room in an ocean steamer, save that it has a desk in it. You are looking at the calendar which hangs beside the mirror. It bears the date the twenty-sixth, and two lines from Swinburne, which you read. Yes, it is on shipboard, for now there rings an alarm of fire, and I hear the rushing of many feet; then the vision fades away."

"The twenty-sixth is very soon, and I never go to sea."

"It will happen as I narrate. To-morrow, word will come to the firm of which you are a member, calling for your presence at some distant point. It will be put off for a time, but one week from to-day you will leave the city by boat—."

"One week!" cried out Rogers, starting up from his chair "why, you clumsy blunderer, you stupid humbug! Don't you see your story does not hang together?"

The stranger sprang up, pressing his thin hands to his face. Then he shook himself like a dog suddenly awakened from a sound sleep, and stared blankly at the merchant.

"One week from to-day is the twenty-seventh," exclaimed Rogers, "and I am to die on the twenty-sixth. I will hear no more of your nonsense. This is a little more than I can tolerate."

"I do not understand you," said the medium in his own voice; "I can not tell what I have been saying to you. I do not even know who spoke through me, but I seem to remember that it was your friend."

Clark Rogers surveyed his visitor for a moment with immeasurable contempt. The man's apparent confusion and his palpable error had snapped the thread by which he held his listener. Rogers, suddenly convinced that his understanding had been led into some sort of an ambush and then overpowered, turned in fury upon the agent of the deceit.

"You may go," he said, restraining himself with difficulty; "if your purpose was to astonish me, I admit that you have succeeded. If you hoped to make me believe that you were in communication with the dead, you have failed. And if you ever again venture, by letter or otherwise, to profane the memory of my friend, I will have you hunted down by the police as a swindling scoundrel."

The stranger was standing near the door of the office. Slowly he raised his arm and pointed his bony index finger at Rogers.

"Remember!" said he.

In another instant he was gone. Rogers seized his pen and began to work on the books which were lying before him, noting down the results of his calculations on a sheet of paper. Frequently he dashed his pen through what he had written and began again. He noticed that his hand trembled and that his fingers with difficulty directed the pen aright, but this he assured himself was the result of intense anger. He understood that he had for a time lost control of himself, and had yielded to what he knew must be superstition, but he was firmly resolved that this should not happen again. Thereupon was begun a struggle between the will power and the natural feelings of Clark Rogers, totally destructive to his peace of mind.

The next day when the firm assembled, as was their custom, to talk over the morning's mail, the senior partner, Mr. Harkness, remarked upon the worn and haggard appearance of Mr. Rogers.

"Rogers is working too hard, I think," said Lyon; "he ought to take a short vacation."

"That is the idea," said Harkness; "you have not been away for many months, now. Why don't you take a little run down to Santa Barbara or San Diego by boat? It is a pleasant enough trip if you are not seasick."

Rogers started and said, rather testily, "What in the world put that into your head? I hate the water, and have never been on an ocean boat in my life."

After some little discussion as to the comparative merits of seasickness and death, the firm began to look over the letters which the corresponding clerk had laid out.

One of these was from a traveling agent of the company, whose route lay in the southern part of the State. It contained the information that a customer of the firm, who was now standing on their books for a number of thousands of dollars, had become badly involved in land speculations, and, it was believed, was on the point of bankruptcy. If the case were handled carefully, the agent considered that most of the debt could be realized, but if the matter was neglected there might be a considerable loss.

"One of us must go down to Ventura immediately, and see what can be done," said Harkness.

"Without a doubt," said Lyon; "here is Rogers's ocean trip all mapped out for him by fate."

"I am very busy, just now," said Rogers slowly, and he began to feel his heart beat with rapid, ponderous strokes; "how soon ought I to go?"

Before the answer came he felt what it was to be.

"There is no very pressing haste, four or five days is soon enough; say the twenty-fifth or the twenty-sixth."

"If I went, I should go by land, I think."

"You can't do that very well at this season of the year. I notice by the papers that the Santa Clara is very high, and the stages run quite irregularly."

"I will not go," said Rogers, bluntly; "that is to say," he added, in some confusion, "if either of you gentlemen can manage to go in my stead."

"Leave the matter to me," said Lyon, good-naturedly, "I know the man well and the place, also. Leave Rogers to his books."

So the conference ended; although, after Rogers had left the room, the other partners commented with surprise upon the vehemence with which he had spoken. As for Rogers, he spent some time endeavoring to convince himself that he would have acted just as he did, had the portent of death not been hanging over him. The idea of an ocean trip was, of course, distasteful to him, and under any circumstances he would have stood out against it. If it were absolutely necessary he could go, but as Lyon was to attend to the matter, he need give it no further thought.

For more than twenty-four hours he succeeded so well in this purpose as to quite surprise himself, for he had begun to lose confidence in his power over his thoughts. In the afternoon of the next day, however, an event occurred which again flooded his mind with unwelcome memories. As he started to rise from his desk he felt a sudden faintness and a violent fluttering at the heart, succeeded, a moment later, by a straining throughout the system and a spasm of pain. He staggered back into his seat, terribly frightened. The paroxysm was over in an instant, and did not return, but the paleness had not left his features a few minutes later when the senior partner entered the room.

Harkness stopped short on seeing Rogers's face, and said: "My dear fellow, you positively look ill. I don't like it at all."

"I am not feeling particularly well," assented Rogers, nervously.

"You are over-working. You must take a rest. Now, look here, Lyon has not been down to-day, and Mrs. Lyon has just called to say that he has another attack of rheumatism, and that it may last him a week or two.

What in the deuce are we to do? Some one must go
down to Ventura. I can't, that is certain. Now, why don't
you go?"

Rogers turned on him and spoke with almost savage
emphasis: "I will go," he said, and repeated it; "I will go;
and it shall be on the twenty-sixth."

Harkness eyed him for a moment in silence.

"You speak in a strange manner," he said, "as though
something were troubling you."

Rogers drew his hand slowly over his eyes.

"Several odd things have happened to me of late," he
confessed; "I can not explain to you what they were, but
they have tempted me to yield to superstitious fancies. I
suppose such things never trouble you."

"Often, often," said the senior member, dropping into
a seat; "but I had imagined that you were altogether too
matter-of-fact to be affected by such folly. For myself, I
have been addicted to that sort of thing so constantly
that I have, at last, formulated a theory on the subject.
Did I ever mention it to you? I hold that a superstition
positively exists for you if you believe in it, but if you
repudiate it, it is dead. If you have the strength of will to
go deliberately and do what the portent, whatever it may
be, warns you against, you are safe from its influence. If
you dodge the event, of course you dodge the calamity.
But now, if, believing in the danger signal, you either
accidentally or thoughtlessly do what you are warned
against, then the omen holds good, because you still
believe in it. Do you catch the idea?"

"I think I do," answered Rogers; and after some more
conversation concerning the affairs of the firm in
Ventura, the partners separated.

It may have been the consolation of the Harkness philosophy which stole over the troubled mind of Mr. Clark
Rogers, or it may have been that the sudden exertion of
his will power reestablished his confidence in himself; at

all events, the perturbed condition of feeling did not return. Twice more the strange sensations at the heart were experienced, but although they caused him anxiety he was not unnerved, as he had been upon the first attack. He determined, however, to see a physician, and learn whether any immediate difficulty was indicated by these symptoms. So completely had he driven the ghostly message from his thoughts, that he did not remember that this visit to the doctor had been predicted, until he stood before the door of the office in the dusk of the evening.

Then, as he rang the bell, a sudden tremor seized him, and for an instant he felt sick and faint. A moment later he regained control of himself, and laughed carelessly as he remembered how absurdly the medium had failed in his effort to describe the physician's appearance.

"Is the doctor in?" he asked of the servant who answered the bell.

"Step into the office, please; and I will speak to him."

The gas had not been lighted, and the office was quite dark. Mr. Rogers seated himself near one of the windows, and presently a man entered at the other side of the room whom he did not recognize, but who he saw by his stature could not be Dr. Bond.

"Excuse me a moment, until I light the gas," said a voice, which sounded familiarly on his ear: "Dr. Bond is out of the city, Mr. Rogers, but I suppose you would just as soon consult with me."

As he spoke, the light flashed up and he stood revealed, a well-known physician and a member of Rogers's own club; a short man, with very bushy eye-brows and a gray mustache.

On the evening of the next day, as Mr. Harkness was dining alone with his wife, he remarked to her that Rogers had received a bad blow that morning.

"Rogers's heir, you know," said he, "is his sister's son,
a young fellow by the name of Westfall. This morning's
papers contained a dispatch to the effect that he had
committed a serious defalcation, and had bolted for
Canada. It is a terrible affair, and I never saw a man so
completely overcome as Rogers was. He seemed unable
to control himself, and has done nothing but brood over
it all day. He had some hope that it was false, but, on
telegraphing for information, the report was entirely
confirmed. By a curious coincidence, he went to see Dr.
Griffith last night, who warned him that there is something the matter with his heart; and that he had best
see to it that his affairs are all in order. He had intended to make a new will, and now this occurrence
upsets all his previous arrangements."

"Whom will he leave his money to, do you suppose?"
asked Mrs. Harkness.

"He told me who his heir would be, for the reason
that he expects to depend upon me to carry out the pro-
visions of the will in case he should die suddenly, but it
was under promise of secrecy. The person is not a relative. It seems there was some sort of a youthful romantic
attachment."

"How odd!" exclaimed the lady; "one would not suspect it of a man like Mr. Rogers."

The next day the will was drawn and attested, and a
temporary sensation of relief took possession of the tortured mind of Clark Rogers. In spite of repeated assur-
ances to the contrary, he had come to accept the
utterances of the alleged spirit as true, and had put into
the will the name of the woman he had once promised to
marry. He endeavored to make himself believe that he
would have done this just the same, had it not been
suggested to him. He had never been without a suspi-
cion that he had misjudged Mary, and this was nothing
but an effort to repair the wrong. Once more he found

distraction in his work, and for a day thrust away the dread of what was to come.

It was late in the afternoon of the twenty-fifth that the panic again seized him, and the courage with which he had determined to meet and overthrow his superstitious fancies suddenly evaporated. The succession of proofs rose before him like the vision of kings to Macbeth. But one part of the message remained unfulfilled: that he should go to sea on the twenty-sixth, and there meet his death. And he was going to meet fate, instead of avoiding the chance of its consummation. No power could carry him on ship-board if he refused to go, and there was no reason why he should not delay the proposed voyage. The doctor had especially warned him to avoid worry and excitement, and by deciding to go on some other date he could save himself this agitation, foolish it was, to be sure, but none the less positive.

He caught eagerly at this comforting subterfuge and was about to go to the senior partner, when that gentleman entered the room with a newspaper in his hand.

"I say, Rogers," he said, "were you expecting to go to-morrow?" Then without waiting for an answer, he continued: " Because you are liable to be disappointed, if you are. There is a boat to-morrow, but I notice that she does not stop at Ventura. From your mentioning the twenty-sixth so positively, I supposed you had looked it up."

"When does my boat go?"

"On the twenty-seventh, the day after to-morrow. I suppose that will be quite as convenient for you."

Rogers burst into an excited laugh.

"What strikes you as so amusing?" inquired Harkness.

"To think," laughed Rogers, "that I should have made all my plans to go, and never looked to see about the boats. For some reason or other, I had an idea that mine would leave on the twenty-sixth."

Throughout the fated day Rogers sat at his desk over his ledgers. Several times he stopped, glanced at the clock and then at the calendar, and smiled. He was quite free from excitement now, and entirely light-hearted. The thought of sudden death which had flitted through his mind at frequent intervals during the last week was far enough away to be quite amusing. He was more affable with his clerks than they had known him to be for years.

At three o'clock Harkness came into the office wearing his hat and overcoat.

"Come along with me," he said; "I am going on an interesting trip which you will enjoy. I have some friends among the officers of the frigate *Mohican,* which is lying at anchor in the bay, and I am going out to be shown about the ship. They will welcome you, too."

"This is the last resort of Fate," thought Rogers; "how superstition does insult a man, when she has him down."

He was seriously tempted to accept the invitation out of mere bravado, for his old firmness of spirit had returned, but reflecting that there were many things which he must attend to in the time that remained, he declined, and the day closed without further event.

On the morning of the twenty-seventh a coast steamer went out the Golden Gate with Clark Rogers as a passenger. The predicted day of his death had come and gone, and he was still a sound man, with prospect of many years of life ahead of him. The mysterious coin-cidences had revealed to him that strange things might happen for which he could not account, but they had stopped short of more dangerous ground. He was now free from the influence of the superstition, and would soon entirely forget it, save that, at times, he would perhaps look back to laugh at his unexpected display of weakness.

Nevertheless, he found himself this morning subject to a strange sort of depression, for which he could not account. It seemed to have no connection with the disagreeable thoughts of the past few days, but was unique and indescribable. He wandered about the ship, trying in vain to get away from the discomfort of this new sensation. It was the reaction, he told himself, of the strain through which he had been passing. Once thrown from its balance his mind would have to be for a time at the mercy of whatever foolish fancies might seize upon it.

As he leaned against the rail, a prey to these moody reflections, some one touched his arm, and he turned to discover a former book-keeper of the firm, wearing the cap and uniform of the purser of the ship.

"Mr. Rogers, I am astonished and delighted to see you, sir," he said. Never in his life had the merchant stood more in need of company. The cordiality with which he returned his former clerk's greeting quite astonished that gentleman.

After they had talked a few minutes, the purser said: "Won't you come to my room, Mr. Rogers? It is a cozy little place. I notice you are not looking well. It is too chilly for you here, is it not?"

The room was small but pleasant. Mr. Rogers occupied a chair by the desk, while the purser sat on the edge of the bed. The latter was a talkative young man, who experienced an unusual degree of pleasure in meeting as an equal his old employer, of whom he had formerly stood in great awe. While listening to his lively prattle, Mr. Rogers's uneasiness gradually vanished.

"This is a sort of a dangerous trip; do you know it?" said the purser.

"Why, how is that?" inquired the merchant, nervously.

"We are carrying about all the gunpowder, and oil, and such combustibles that the policy will allow. If we should catch fire now, it would not take long to blow us skyward. But I ought not to talk to you of such matters; you might not sleep well at night after it."

Mr. Rogers said but little, not being by nature a very companionable man. With the purser it was different; it was not often that he secured so attentive a listener as his present one.

"Are you going to stop in Ventura very long?" he inquired.

"No," answered the other.

"Well, you ought to," said the purser; "everything is beautiful down there now. The hills are a velvety green, and the meadows are fairly carpeted with wild flowers. Spring begins a little earlier than it does up above, and it is already well under way.

> 'For winter's rains and ruins are over,
> And all the season of snows and sins.'

"I suppose you do not care much for poetry but I am very fond of it, and try to commit some to memory every day; to use for quotations, you know. Those lines are from Swinburne."

"Swinburne," repeated Rogers, mechanically. Then he gave a quick glance about the room, and his face turned a shade pale. Here was the desk, the white painted walls, and the mirror.

The purser stood up, interrupting his thoughts.

"Yes," he said; "I am very fond of Swinburne; so much so that I keep a calendar in my room with a selection for each day of the year. By Jove! That reminds me! Yesterday I didn't——"

He placed his hand on a coat which hung over the desk beside the mirror, and was about to remove it, when the officer of the deck stepped to the door.

"Hall," he said, "you are wanted;" and then added in an undertone which Rogers heard quite plainly, "trouble down below."

The purser went quickly out, closing the screen door behind him. Rogers started up and drew the coat to one side. Beneath it was the calendar bearing in large red letters the number twenty-six and the lines:

"In his heart is a blind desire,
In his eyes foreknowledge of death,"

The words seemed to sear his eyeballs as he read them, and he staggered back, gasping for breath. At that instant he heard the clang of the fire-alarm bell, the cries of the sailors, and the rushing of many people along the deck. He sank to the floor, his lips parted in the effort to speak a name.

When the purser returned, after adjusting the difficulty for which he had been summoned below, he noticed the men putting up the hose at the conclusion of the fire-drill, and wondered if the sudden call had startled his guest. Upon the floor of the room he found Clark Rogers, his stern features black and distorted in death.

Reprinted from The Argonaut, *June 13, 1888.*

Beyond The Wall

by Ambrose Bierce

Many years ago, on my way from Hongkong to New York, I passed a week in San Francisco. A long time had gone by since I had been in that city, during which my ventures in the Orient had prospered beyond my hope; I was rich and could afford to revisit my own country to renew my friendship with such of the companions of my youth as still lived and remembered me with the old affection. Chief of these, I hoped, was Mohun Dampier, an old schoolmate with whom I had held a desultory correspondence which had long ceased, as is the way of correspondence between men. You may have observed that the indisposition to write a merely social letter is in the ratio of the square of the distance between you and your correspondent. It is a law.

I remembered Dampier as a handsome, strong young fellow of scholarly tastes, with an aversion to work and a marked indifference to many of the things that the world cares for, including wealth, of which, however, he had inherited enough to put him beyond the reach of want. In his family, one of the oldest and most aristocratic in the country, it was, I think, a matter of pride that no member of it had ever been in neither trade nor politics, nor suffered any kind of distinction. Mohun was a trifle sentimental, and had in him a singular element of superstition, which led him to the study of all manner of occult subjects, although his sane mental health safeguarded him against fantastic and perilous faiths. He made daring incursions into the realm of the unreal without renouncing his residence in the partly surveyed and charted region of what we are pleased to call certitude.

The night of my visit to him was stormy. The Californian winter was on, and the incessant rain plashed in the deserted streets, or, lifted by irregular gusts of wind, was hurled against the houses with incredible fury. With no small difficulty my cabman found the right place, away out toward the ocean beach, in a sparsely populated suburb. The dwelling, a rather ugly one, apparently, stood in the center of its grounds, which as nearly as I could make out in the gloom were destitute of either flowers or grass. Three or four trees, writhing and moaning in the torment of the tempest, appeared to be trying to escape from their dismal environment and take the chance of finding a better one out at sea. The house was a two-story brick structure with a tower, a story higher, at one corner. In a window of that was the only visible light. Something in the appearance of the place made me shudder, a performance that may have been assisted by a rill of rain-water down my back as I scuttled to cover in the doorway.

In answer to my note apprising him of my wish to call, Dampier had written, "Don't ring—open the door and come up." I did so. The staircase was dimly lighted by a single gas-jet at the top of the second flight. I managed to reach the landing without disaster and entered by an open door into the lighted square room of the tower. Dampier came forward in gown and slippers to receive me, giving me the greeting that I wished, and if I had held a thought that it might more fitly have been accorded me at the front door the first look at him dispelled any sense of his inhospitality.

He was not the same. Hardly past middle age, he had gone gray and had acquired a pronounced stoop. His figure was thin and angular, his face deeply lined, his complexion dead-white, without a touch of color. His eyes, unnaturally large, glowed with a fire that was almost uncanny.

He seated me, proffered a cigar, and with grave and obvious sincerity assured me of the pleasure that it gave him to meet me. Some unimportant conversation followed, but all the while I was dominated by a melancholy sense of the great change in him. This he must have perceived, for he suddenly said with a bright enough smile, "You are disappointed in me—*non sum qualis eram.*"[1]

I hardly knew what to reply, but managed to say: "Why, really, I don't know: your Latin is about the same."

He brightened again. "No," he said, "being a dead language, it grows in appropriateness. But please have the patience to wait: where I am going there is perhaps a better tongue. Will you care to have a message in it?"

The smile faded as he spoke, and as he concluded he was looking into my eyes with a gravity that distressed me. Yet I would not surrender myself to his mood, nor permit him to see how deeply his prescience of death affected me.

"I fancy that it will be long," I said, "before human speech will cease to serve our need; and then the need, with its possibilities of service, will have passed."

He made no reply, and I too was silent, for the talk had taken a dispiriting turn, yet I knew not how to give it a more agreeable character. Suddenly, in a pause of the storm, when the dead silence was almost startling by contrast with the previous uproar, I heard a gentle tapping, which appeared to come from the wall behind my chair. The sound was such as might have been made

---

1. "I am not what I once was."

by a human hand, not as upon a door by one asking
admittance, but rather, I thought, as an agreed signal,
an assurance of someone's presence in an adjoining
room; most of us, I fancy, have had more experience of
such communications than we should care to relate.
I glanced at Dampier. If possibly there was something
of amusement in the look he did not observe it. He
appeared to have forgotten my presence, and was staring at the wall behind me with an expression in his eyes
that I am unable to name, although my memory of it is
as vivid to-day as was my sense of it then. The situation
was embarrassing; I rose to take my leave. At this he
seemed to recover himself.

"Please be seated," he said; "it is nothing—no one is
there." But the tapping was repeated, and with the same
gentle, slow insistence as before.

"Pardon me," I said, "it is late. May I call to-morrow?"

He smiled—a little mechanically, I thought. "It is very
delicate of you," said he, "but quite needless. Really, this
is the only room in the tower, and no one is there. At
least—" He left the sentence incomplete, rose, and threw
up a window, the only opening in the wall from which
the sound seemed to come. "See."

Not clearly knowing what else to do I followed him to
the window and looked out. A street-lamp some little
distance away gave enough light through the murk of
the rain that was again falling in torrents to make it
entirely plain that "no one was there." In truth there was
nothing but the sheer blank wall of the tower.

Dampier closed the window and signing me to my
seat resumed his own.

The incident was not in itself particularly mysterious;
anyone of a dozen explanations was possible (though
none has occurred to me), yet it impressed me strangely,
the more, perhaps, from my friend's effort to reassure
me, which seemed to dignify it with a certain

significance and importance. He had proved that no one
was there, but in that fact lay all the interest; and he
proffered no explanation. His silence was irritating and
made me resentful.

"My good friend," I said, somewhat ironically, I fear,
"I am not disposed to question your right to harbor as
many spooks as you find agreeable to your taste and
consistent with your notions of companionship; that is
no business of mine. But being just a plain man of
affairs, mostly of this world, I find spooks needless to
my peace and comfort. I am going to my hotel, where my
fellow-guests are still in the flesh."

It was not a very civil speech, but he manifested no
feeling about it. "Kindly remain," he said: "I am grateful
for your presence here. What you have heard to-night I
believe myself to have heard twice before. Now I *know* it
was no illusion. That is much to me—more than you
know. Have a fresh cigar and a good stock of patience
while I tell you the story."

The rain was now falling more steadily, with a low,
monotonous susurration, interrupted at long intervals
by the sudden slashing of the boughs of the trees as the
wind rose and failed. The night was well advanced, but
both sympathy and curiosity held me a willing listener
to my friend's monologue, which I did not interrupt by a
single word from beginning to end.

"Ten years ago," he said, "I occupied a ground-floor
apartment in one of a row of houses, all alike, away at
the other end of the town, on what we call Rincon Hill.
This had been the best quarter of San Francisco, but
had fallen into neglect and decay, partly because the
primitive character of its domestic architecture no longer suited the maturing tastes of our wealthy citizens,
partly because certain public improvements had made
a wreck of it. The row of dwellings in one of which I
lived stood a little way back from the street, each having

a miniature garden, separated from its neighbors by low iron fences and bisected with mathematical precision by a box-bordered gravel walk from gate to door.[2]

"One morning as I was leaving my lodging I observed a young girl entering the adjoining garden on the left. It was a warm day in June, and she was lightly gowned in white. From her shoulders hung a broad straw hat profusely decorated with flowers and wonderfully beribboned in the fashion of the time. My attention was not long held by the exquisite simplicity of her costume, for no one could look at her face and think of anything earthly. Do not fear; I shall not profane it by description; it was beautiful exceedingly. All that I had ever seen or dreamed of loveliness was in that matchless living picture by the hand of the Divine Artist. So deeply did it move me that, without a thought of the impropriety of the act, I unconsciously bared my head, as a devout Catholic or well-bred Protestant uncovers before an image of the Blessed Virgin. The maiden showed no displeasure; she merely turned her glorious dark eyes upon me with a look that made me catch my breath, and without other recognition of my act passed into the house. For a moment I stood motionless, hat in hand, painfully conscious of my rudeness, yet so dominated by the emotion inspired by that vision of incomparable beauty that my penitence was less poignant than it should have been. Then I went my way, leaving my heart behind. In the natural course of things I should probably have remained away until nightfall, but by the

2. The "public improvements" Bierce mentions refer to the "Second Street Cut" of 1869, which gouged a level path through Rincon Hill along Second Street. The 75-foot chasm it created, leaving houses on both sides in danger of toppling into it, led to Rincon Hill's decline as an elite residential district.

middle of the afternoon I was back in the little garden,
affecting an interest in the few foolish flowers that I had
never before observed. My hope was vain; she did not
appear.

"To a night of unrest succeeded a day of expectation
and disappointment, but on the day after, as I wandered
aimlessly about the neighborhood, I met her. Of course I
did not repeat my folly of uncovering, nor venture by
even so much as too long a look to manifest an interest
in her; yet my heart was beating audibly. I trembled and
consciously colored as she turned her big black eyes
upon me with a look of obvious recognition entirely
devoid of boldness or coquetry.

"I will not weary you with particulars; many times
afterward I met the maiden, yet never either addressed
her or sought to fix her attention. Nor did I take any
action toward making her acquaintance. Perhaps my
forbearance, requiring so supreme an effort of
self-denial, will not be entirely clear to you. That I was
heels over head in love is true, but who can overcome
his habit of thought, or reconstruct his character?

"I was what some foolish persons are pleased to call,
and others, more foolish, are pleased to be called—an
aristocrat; and despite her beauty, her charms and
graces, the girl was not of my class. I had learned her
name—which it is needless to speak—and something of
her family. She was an orphan, a dependent niece of the
impossible elderly fat woman in whose lodging-house
she lived. My income was small and I lacked the talent
for marrying; it is perhaps a gift. An alliance with that
family would condemn me to its manner of life, part me
from my books and studies, and in a social sense reduce
me to the ranks. It is easy to deprecate such consider-
ations as these and I have not retained myself for the
defense. Let judgment be entered against me, but in
strict justice all my ancestors for generations should be

made co-defendants and I be permitted to plead in miti-
gation of punishment the imperious mandate of hered-
ity. To a mesalliance of that kind every globule of my
ancestral blood spoke in opposition. In brief, my tastes,
habits, instinct, with whatever of reason my love had left
me—all fought against it. Moreover, I was an irreclaim-
able sentimentalist, and found a subtle charm in an
impersonal and spiritual relation which acquaintance
might vulgarize and marriage would certainly dispel.
No woman, I argued, is what this lovely creature seems.
Love is a delicious dream; why should I bring about my
own awakening?

"The course dictated by all this sense and sentiment
was obvious. Honor, pride, prudence, preservation of my
ideals—all commanded me to go away, but for that I was
too weak. The utmost that I could do by a mighty effort
of will was to cease meeting the girl, and that I did. I
even avoided the chance encounters of the garden, leaving my lodging only when I knew that she had gone to
her music lessons, and returning after nightfall. Yet all
the while I was as one in a trance, indulging the most
fascinating fancies and ordering my entire intellectual
life in accordance with my dream. Ah, my friend, as one
whose actions have a traceable relation to reason, you
cannot know the fool's paradise in which I lived.

"One evening the devil put it into my head to be an
unspeakable idiot. By apparently careless and purpose-
less questioning I learned from my gossipy landlady that
the young woman's bedroom adjoined my own, a
party-wall between. Yielding to a sudden and coarse
impulse I gently rapped on the wall. There was no
response, naturally, but I was in no mood to accept a
rebuke. A madness was upon me and I repeated the
folly, the offense, but again ineffectually, and I had the
decency to desist.

"An hour later, while absorbed in some of my
infernal studies, I heard, or thought I heard, my signal
answered. Flinging down my books I sprang to the wall
and as steadily as my beating heart would permit gave
three slow taps upon it. This time the response was distinct, unmistakable: one, two, three—an exact repetition
of my signal. That was all I could elicit, but it was
enough—too much.

"The next evening, and for many evenings afterward,
that folly went on, I always having 'the last word.' During the whole period I was deliriously happy, but with
the perversity of my nature I persevered in my resolution
not to see her. Then, as I should have expected, I got no
further answers. 'She is disgusted,' I said to myself,
'with what she thinks my timidity in making no more
definite advances'; and I resolved to seek her and make
her acquaintance and—what? I did not know, nor do I
now know, what might have come of it. I know only that
I passed days and days trying to meet her, and all in
vain; she was invisible as well as inaudible. I haunted
the streets where we had met, but she did not come.
From my window I watched the garden in front of her
house, but she passed neither in nor out. I fell into the
deepest dejection, believing that she had gone away, yet
took no steps to resolve my doubt by inquiry of my landlady, to whom, indeed, I had taken an unconquerable
aversion from her having once spoken of the girl with
less of reverence then I thought befitting.

"There came a fateful night. Worn out with emotion,
irresolution and despondency, I had retired early and
fallen into such sleep as was still possible to me. In the
middle of the night something—some malign power bent
upon the wrecking of my peace forever—caused me to
open my eyes and sit up, wide awake and listening
intently for I knew not what. Then I thought I heard a
faint tapping on the wall—the mere ghost of the familiar

signal. In a few moments it was repeated: one, two, three—no louder than before, but addressing a sense alert and strained to receive it. I was about to reply when the Adversary of Peace again intervened in my affairs with a rascally suggestion of retaliation. She had long and cruelly ignored me; now I would ignore her. Incredible fatuity—may God forgive it! All the rest of the night I lay awake, fortifying my obstinacy with shame- less justifications and—listening.

"Late the next morning, as I was leaving the house, I met my landlady, entering.

"'Good morning, Mr. Dampier,' she said. 'Have you heard the news?' "I replied in words that I had heard no news; in manner, that I did not care to hear any. The manner escaped her observation.

"'About the sick young lady next door,' she babbled on. 'What! you did not know? Why, she has been ill for weeks. And now—'

"I almost sprang upon her. 'And now,' I cried, 'now what?'

"'She is dead.'

"That is not the whole story. In the middle of the night, as I learned later, the patient, awakening from a long stupor after a week of delirium, had asked—it was her last utterance—that her bed be moved to the oppo- site side of the room. Those in attendance had thought the request a vagary of her delirium, but had complied. And there the poor passing soul had exerted its failing will to restore a broken connection—a golden thread of sentiment between its innocence and a monstrous base- ness owning a blind, brutal allegiance to the Law of Self.

"What reparation could I make? Are there masses that can be said for the repose of souls that are abroad such nights as this—spirits 'blown about by the viewless winds'—coming in the storm and darkness with signs and portents, hints of memory and presages of doom?

"This is the third visitation. On the first occasion I
was too skeptical to do more than verify by natural
methods the character of the incident; on the second, I
responded to the signal after it had been several times
repeated, but without result. To-night's recurrence
completes the 'fatal triad' expounded by Parapelius
Necromantius.[3] There is no more to tell."

When Dampier had finished his story I could think of
nothing relevant that I cared to say, and to question him
would have been a hideous impertinence. I rose and
bade him good night in a way to convey to him a sense
of my sympathy, which he silently acknowledged by a
pressure of the hand. That night, alone with his sorrow
and remorse, he passed into the Unknown.

Reprinted from Bierce's collection "Can Such Things Be?"
(1893).

---

3. Parapelius Necromantius is apparently a made up name.

A Mirage Of Murder
The Strange Happenings in No. 4313 Pacific Street.

by Howard Markle Hoke

Pacific Street starts in the slums, and runs across the city. The highest number upon it is 8626, and the house with which this narrative deals is No. 4313. It stands, therefore, exactly half-way between the abodes of poverty and wealth.[1] At the time of the occurrence herein to be related, it was kept as a lodging and boarding- place for men by Mrs. James Prowitt, whose long experience had made her keen and wary. Her guests were of all classes and descriptions, men rising from the lower street frequently meeting at her table those who were descending from the gentility of the avenue.

One October morning a young man applied to her for a room. She set her little gray eyes sharply upon him, as was her habit, but saw nothing out of the commonplace. She always divided her patrons into three classes—those coming up from near the bay, those sinking from the avenue, and the stationary middle class. She shrewdly placed this one among the second class, but that made little difference to her. He was medium in size, with a frank face and a manner which gave her the impression that he knew what he was about, and was exceedingly wide-awake in doing it. He said he was a traveling man, could furnish good references, and gave his name as Harry Mulford.

---

1. These are fictional addresses, since today's Pacific Avenue ends in the 3200 block. Hoke had the sociology right, though: lower Pacific (still called Pacific <u>Street</u>) was part of the notorious Barbary Coast, whereas the higher addresses are part of the exclusive residential enclave of Pacific Heights.

"My third-floor front is vacant," Mrs. Prowitt said, "but I usually get fifteen dollars a month for it."

"That is entirely satisfactory," Mulford replied. "The price is nothing to me, although I shall not occupy the room more than one night a month. But I shall want it kept ready for me, though you are at liberty to use it any night, provided you do not receive word of my coming before six o'clock. I shall pay you in advance, sending you your money by mail on the last of each month." He drew out his purse, counted fifteen dollars upon his knee, and added, "Here is the first month's rent, provided you will let me have the room."

Mrs. Prowitt was too keen to let such a chance slip, and she quickly closed the transaction. Her requirement of references had always been a mere form—often a ruse to get rid of an unpromising applicant. She did not, therefore, ask Mulford for his, considering his money sufficient indorsement.

"It is probable," said Mulford, as he delivered the money and rose to leave, "that I shall not reappear for several months, and if you do not receive fifteen dollars from me near the first of any month, you will be at liberty to rent the room. It is likely that I may send some one occasionally to occupy the room, but he will always bring a note from me."

This piece of luck was too good for Mrs. Prowitt to keep to herself, and it was soon a matter for general discussion around her tables. A man who could afford to pay for a room without occupying it was a rarity at No. 4313, and Mulford became a mystery. The first month passed, and the third-floor front was unoccupied, except when Mrs. Prowitt quartered a transient. On the last day of this month, a registered letter was delivered to her, from which she drew three crisp five-dollar bills and a note from Mulford, stating that he would soon send a friend to take possession of the room. But when

this and several more months passed without other sign
or representative of Mulford than the regular letters
inclosing the bills, the rental of the upper chamber
became a sensation.

At last, however, one early December afternoon a little
old man appeared, bringing from Mulford a note which
stated his wish that Mrs. Prowitt would place in his
room the article that the bearer would deliver, and to
have the apartment kept ready for occupancy. The little
old man was quite odd. He was much bent and very
gray. His left eye was blind; but the right, restless and
twinkling, together with his whole countenance, made
Mrs. Prowitt think he could tell a great deal, if so
minded. He was not so minded, however, and her questions elicited only amusement, to which his blindness
lent the appearance of continual winking.

The article he brought was a large, three-fold, Japanese screen, highly decorated with gilt birds, reptiles,
and animals disporting themselves on a sable ground.
After the little old man had gone, and Mrs. Prowitt had
set the screen in Mulford's room, she went down to the
tables to express her opinion that a Japanese screen
was a queer article for a young man to send, and the
boarders agreed with her so strongly as to repair to the
apartment to inspect it. The screen was ordinary, yet
extraordinary, and curiosity played about the bamboo
frame as whimsically as the golden decorations within
it. A satchel, or a trunk, or even a chair would have
aroused simple expectation; but a Japanese screen,
though not uncommon in a bedroom, suggested something so decidedly out of the common-place that
Mulford's advent was awaited with lively interest. A
week passed, however; and, though Mrs. Prowitt kept
gas burning in the evenings, had fresh water put daily
into the pitcher, and hung clean towels upon the rack,
neither Mulford nor his friend appeared.

For twelve days she had these preparations made; but upon the thirteenth Mulford's friend came. It was half-past eight when the maid admitted him to the parlor. At this hour all the lodgers were out pursuing their various evening pastimes, except John Baylor, who was practicing upon his clarinet in his second-floor room. Mrs. Prowitt went to the parlor, expecting to find a young man of about Mulford's age, but she was surprised to see a gentleman of probably sixty. He was, however, well preserved and active, and was dressed very much better than anyone she had ever lodged. There was an unmistakable air of the avenue about him that set Mrs. Prowitt to thinking she had seen him before, and to wondering where it had been. He carried a bulging blue bag of heavy material, and his whole bearing and appearance were those of a busy lawyer. Mrs. Prowitt made these observations distinctly, as was her habit; but later occurrences indented them in her mind. In relating exactly how the old lawyer entered the parlor, how he talked, and in describing him, she always had difficulty putting one fact into words.

"Somehow," she always said, "he made me creep. He sat right in front of me and he seemed to be there like any other man, but there was something or other about him that made him seem unreal, a kind of a strange shadow of a rich old man I had seen upon the avenue. His voice, too, sounded kind of unnatural; something like an echo of a real voice speaking away off somewhere. I thought at first that he was only absent-minded, but the more I looked at him, the more plainly I saw that there was something about him I could not explain, and can't now."

He gave her a note in Mulford's hand, merely introducing him as the friend who desired to occupy his room for the night, and he would consider it a favor if

Mrs. Prowitt would make him comfortable and let him have all he might wish.

"Is there anything you want me particularly to do?" Mrs. Prowitt asked him. She has always laid great stress upon the fact that she observed everything that occurred that night accurately and has been unvarying in her narrative.

"Is there a table in the room?" the lawyer asked absently.

"Yes; Mr. Mulford requested me to put one in for him."

"That is well. Then all I wish is to be entirely undisturbed. I have many papers to examine to-night," he said, tapping the blue bag. "I am engaged on a matter of vast importance to a wealthy estate, and I shall ask you to see that no one is admitted to the room. I am ready to go to work now, if you please."

Mrs. Prowitt showed him to the third-floor front, turned up the light, and before leaving, saw him take from the bag a large bundle of papers, tied with pink tape, and lay them busily upon the table. He then pulled up a chair and sat down. She noticed particularly that the Japanese screen stood about three feet from the back of his chair and about two feet from the windows. The weather being cold, the sashes were down and locked, and the lower inside shutters drawn and latched. There was a sheer descent from the windows to the pavement, with no outside ledge below them, so that it was impossible for anyone to have entered the room through them. Mrs. Prowitt has been unwavering in this statement, as well as in declaring that no one was hidden behind the screen or elsewhere in the room when she admitted the lawyer.

It was only a few minutes after nine when she left the old man intently engaged over his papers. On her way downstairs, she stopped in Mr. Baylor's room to tell him that Mulford's friend had come. She did so, she has said, not because they had all looked for him so long, but because the man had given her a queer feeling of dread that she could not throw off. She naturally wondered what could have brought so rich a lawyer to her house; but it was not this query that made her uneasy. She told Baylor of this strange impression, and of the fact that, while with the old lawyer in the room, she had had a creepy notion that she was entirely alone, although he had been plain to her eyes. She had noticed that he had walked vigorously, but his steps had been surprisingly faint, and the papers had not rattled when he took them from the bag. She was very nervous. She did not believe in ghosts, she declared, but certainly this was the strangest lodger she had ever had in her house. She was afraid something dreadful might happen, and she asked Baylor to keep his door open and to walk up the stairway occasionally and listen. He promised to do so, and she left him.

At eleven o'clock she hurried back and said:

"Would you mind going with me to Mr. Mulford's room and listen outside the door? I want to know whether that old man is sleeping. I see from the pavement outside that he has turned the gas out."

"That cannot be," Baylor answered, excitedly. "I walked up the stairs not more than five minutes ago and saw his light shining through the transom."

"Saw his light?" echoed Mrs. Prowitt, in an awed whisper. "It was just about five minutes ago that I looked from the pavement outside and his windows were dark. Are you sure you saw the light?"

"Yes; but I could not hear a sound inside the room."

"Mr. Baylor, there is something terrible in the air to-night, and I can't tell what it is. Let us go up there and listen."

They ascended to Mulford's room. Bright light was shining through the transom. Mrs. Prowitt knocked three times, but received no answer. Then she called, but the room remained perfectly silent.

"I would like you to look over the transom, Mr. Baylor," she said. "There is something mysterious here."

Baylor brought to the door two chairs that were standing in the hall, and stepping upon one, looked through the transom. He started, and asked Mrs. Prowitt to get up on the other and look. They saw the old lawyer still sitting at the table with bundles of legal papers before him. He was too deeply engaged to notice that his long gray hair had slipped down over his forehead and almost overhung his eyes. As they looked from his peaceful face to the documents before him, Mrs. Prowitt started violently, caught Baylor's arm, and said:

"Look at his hands. He is making the motions of writing, but there is no pen in his hand. He is——"

She faltered from fright, and Baylor said:

"He is a madman, Mrs. Prowitt."

"No, he is worse than that. He is not a real man. Something awful is going to happen to-night. I did not quite trust that man Mulford from the start. Why should he have rented this room and not occupied it, if everything had been right? This is terrible. Look there. Did you see the screen move?"

"No, I did not, but——"

He stopped abruptly, for two hands rose from behind the screen, and, catching its extreme ends, lifted it from the floor and carried it stealthily toward the old man. They were large and muscular, ugly and grimy—such hands as would delve in the slime and vice of the lower street. With the exception of his hands, the person behind the screen was hidden until he had carried it, noiselessly and stealthily, until it almost touched the old man's chair. There the hands stopped it and stood it

securely, and instantly a head rose from behind it. The
terrible face held the two outside watchers motionless.
The vileness and wickedness of the slums was ground
into each blotched and bloated feature. The terrible
creature looked for some minutes upon the old lawyer
with a leer of murderous triumph. Then, with a horrible
smile of satisfaction, the man raised his right arm high
over the screen, his dirty, talon-like hand clutching a
dagger.

Mrs. Prowitt shrank with a scream from the sight,
and fell to a sitting posture upon her chair; while
Baylor, aroused to action, pounded upon the glass of the
transom and kicked upon the door, but the old lawyer
continued peacefully writing at the table, and the assassin was not stayed in his purpose. With a swift, skillful
stroke, the knife fell, and Baylor saw it sink into the
lawyer's breast, saw him writhe upon the chair and fall
to the floor. He leaped from the chair and threw himself
against the door, but it withstood his force.

"Help me here, Mrs. Prowitt," he cried. "The lawyer
has been murdered. The door is locked upon the inside.
Help me break it in."

Their united strength at last broke the lock, and the
door swung in. Baylor took one rapid step forward, but
stopped upon the sill with a startled cry. The room was
dark and silent. No moan or sound of death-struggling
came from the murdered man under the table.

"A match, Mrs. Prowitt," he said; "for the love of
heaven, let us have a light here!"

"There is a match-safe over the wash-stand in the
corner," gasped the landlady.

For a few moments Baylor groped in the blackness for
a match. At last he struck one, and the gas puffed up.
He shrank back against the wall by the door. The room
was entirely deserted; the table was bare of legal papers;
the screen stood in its place near the window; and there

was no body of a murdered man upon the floor, or any blood or other trace of him. The room was precisely as it had been before the lawyer came.

In the midst of an animated discussion, at Mrs. Prowitt's table next morning, of the strange crime, one of the boarders, who had already breakfasted and gone out, rushed back with a paper, which, under display head-lines, told of the brutal murder of Abel Christiansea, one of the city's noted lawyers. It detailed how he had been sitting in the study at his home on the avenue, going over some valuable papers in the matter of a vast estate in litigation. The murderer had entered through a window, had crept upon Mr. Christiansea under cover of a Japanese screen that stood behind his chair, and had struck him to the heart with a dagger. The assassin, who had escaped with all the papers, was said to be one of the most dangerous criminals of the slums.

About ten o'clock on this same morning, the little old man who had brought the Japanese screen appeared at No. 4313, saying that Mr. Mulford had sent him for it.

"I don't know that I ought to let you have it," said Mrs. Prowitt.

"Why not?" asked the little old man, with a queer twinkle of his unblinded eye.

"There was a terrible murder on the avenue last night by a man who stabbed a lawyer from behind a Japanese screen, and me and one of my lodgers saw the vision of a man come from behind Mr. Mulford's screen and kill a strange old man who had come as Mr. Mulford's friend."

"It is certainly remarkable," said the little old man, winking his blind eye; "but you certainly won't keep Mr. Mulford's screen just because you saw a vision?"

"Go up for it then, for I won't touch it," said Mrs. Prowitt. "I will be glad to have the terrible thing out of my house. If I wasn't afraid of it, I would not let you have it."

When the little old man reappeared, carrying the screen, she said:

"If I could see how there could be any connection between this screen and the one on the avenue, I would keep you here and send for the police."

"I don't see what possible connection there could be," said the little old man, ducking his head sidewise, and squinting at her quizzically. "If I could, I wouldn't ask you for the screen. But I will ask Mr. Mulford, and if there is, of course I'll come around and tell you. By the way, he says you need not keep the room for him any longer."

And picking up the screen, he briskly walked away.

Reprinted from The Argonaut, *February 4, 1895.*

Who Believes in Ghosts!

by Jack London

"A remarkably good one—for you; but I know of one
that beats—" "No, no, Damon. I know you always have a
story to cap the last one; but I meant this in all honesty,
and if you doubt its truth, at least believe my sincerity
in telling it."

"George! You don't mean to tell me that you really
believe in ghosts? Why, the very idea is absurd, and to
connect credence in such a thing with you is—is—"
and Van Buster, otherwise known as Damon, paused
for lack of an expletive, and finally exploded in
"Preposterous!"[1]

"But I do believe in it, and in my faith I am not alone,
for on my side I can array the greatest lights of every age
from the days of Chaldean necromancy[2] down to the
cold, scientific 'to day.' Pause and reflect, O Damon and
Pythias, too, for I can see the skeptical twinkle in your
eye. Remember that in every time, in every land, and in
every people, there have been and there are many who
did believe in the soul's return after death. Can you,
with this great mass of evidence staring you in the face,
say that it is all the creation of diseased brains and
abnormal imaginations?" And as Damon and Pythias
both affirmed his accusation, he concluded with a pious

1. London named his lead characters Damon and Pythias after
   two youths of Greek folklore who were loyal and inseparable
   friends. He did this no doubt to heighten their bond and make
   the evil possession that seizes them that much more believable.
2. The use of magic powers of the dead by the Chaldeans, a
   Semitic people of ancient Babylonia.

hope that some day they would be forced to change their minds by a proof very unpleasantly applied.

"Come, come, Pythias! What have you to say in our mutual defense? Show our credulous friend the firm foundation on which we stand. Bring all your mighty logic to bear, and sophistry, too, for it is a very bad case. Show him that this psychic force is but the creation of man's too fertile imagination; prove to him that these earth-bound spirits, astral forms and disembodied entities are but chimeras!"

"Ah, Damon," he lazily drawled, "I care not to waste my stupendous knowledge and laborious research on such petty subjects. If I were challenged into controversy on the land, tariff or finance question, I fain would reply; but this seems too much like the nursery babble on the bogie man. Earth-bound spirits forsooth! All I can say to dear George is that he is an ass, and until he can introduce me to some astral form, I dismiss the subject."

In no wise put out by the sarcasm of his friends, George said: "I feel like singing that old doggerel—

'Just go down to Derby town,
And see the same as I.'

For I have seen many, and what I consider authentic, proofs of the existence and activity of this force. I know that all argument is useless when I have opposed to me, two such master minds; yet so far have they sank into intellectual stagnation, that they know not, and know not that they know not.

"We all view the world through colored glasses; but their glasses are so very, very green, that one almost feels—"

"And you must confess that yours are rather smoky," interrupted Damon. "But come, George, we'll not quarrel over such a subject. You know the position I always assume when dealing with the unknown. I neither affirm nor deny, and I can but say that plausibility, if not possibility, is with your belief. In justice to you, to myself and to the world, all I can say is that I do not know, but would like to know. And I coincide with Pythias in asking you to bring us personally in contact with these disembodied souls."

"There's the old Birchall mansion," drawled Pythias; "perhaps we can gain an introduction there. They say it's haunted."

"The very place!" cried Damon. "Do you think the 'ghost' that walks the gloomy corridors at midnight's dread hour, etc., would condescend to become visible for the edification of two such miserable, unbelieving mortals as we are? Here's a grand opportunity—it's only ten, and we can be there by eleven. Pythias and I will arm ourselves with a couple of dozen candles, half a dozen ounces of Durham, and *Trilby* to read aloud turn about,—the last to affect and prepare our imaginations. What say you, Pythias, to the lark?"

"I am always agreeable," he replied. "I've got the time to spare now from my grind. I'm through with the ex'es, you know. But I move to amend by striking out *Trilby* and inserting chess. Also that we bring a bunch of fire-crackers to let off when the ghost makes his appearance. It might be a Chinese devil, you know. And of course you'll accompany us, George? No? Then you had better find a companion and keep guard outside in case of accidents, and to see that we do not run away."

"That's easily arranged," answered George. "I can get Fred. He will just be going out now to hunt cats."

"Hunt cats!" from Damon and Pythias.

"Yes, hunt cats. You see, he's deep in Gray's *Anatomy* now, and is hard run for subjects. Why, he even did away with his sister's big Maltese, and so proud was he when he had articulated it, that he had the cheek to

show it to her, telling her it was the skeleton of a
rabbit."

"The brute!"

"The cat?"

"No, Fred. How poor Dora must have mourned for her
lost tabby."

"He ought to be thrashed."

"No, dissected, then articulated and presented to his
bereaved relatives as a missing link. They would no
more recognize him than did Dora her cat."

"If cats had souls I would be afraid to venture out at
night if I were he. Have they got souls, George?"

"I don't know; but don't let's waste any more time, if
we intend carrying this project out. We must all meet by
eleven sharp, in front of the house."

They agreed. So paying their reckoning, they left the
restaurant—George to hunt up Fred, and Damon and
Pythias to invest their spare cash in candles, fire-crackers and Durham.

By eleven, the four friends had assembled in front of
the Birchall mansion. They were all high-spirited, and
when they came to part, George addressed them as
follows:

"O Damon, the agnostic, and Pythias, the skeptic,
heed well my last words. Ye venture within a place purported by the vulgar to be haunted. The truth of this as
yet remains to be proven; but remember that this power,
which you will have to contend with, will not be resisted
as those earthly forces of which you have knowledge. It
is mysterious, imponderable and powerful; it is invisible,
yet oftentimes visible; and it can exert itself in innumer-
able ways. Opening locked doors, putting out lights,
dropping bricks, and strange sounds, cries, curses and
moans, are but the lower demonstrations of this phenomena. Also, as we have in this life men inclined to
good and evil, so have we, in the life to come, spirits,

both good and bad. Woe betide you if you are thrown in contact with evil spirits. You may be lifted up bodily and dashed to the floor or against the walls like a football; you may see grewsome sights even beyond the conception of mortal; and so great a terror may be brought upon you, that your minds may lose their balance and leave you gibbering idiots or violently insane. And again, these evil spirits have the power to deprive you of one, two or all of your senses, if they so wish. They can burst your ear-drums; sear your eyes; destroy your voice; sadly impair your sense of taste and smell, and paralyze the body in any or every nerve. And even as in the days of Christ, they may make their habitation within your bodies, and you will be tormented with evil spirits, and then—the asylum and padded cell stares you in the face. I have no advice to give you in dealing with this mysterious subject, for I am ignorant; but my parting words are, 'keep cool; may you prosper in your undertaking, and beware!'"

They then separated—Damon and Pythias in quest of ghosts, and George and Fred in quest of cats.

The first couple strode up to the front door; but finding it locked, and that the spirits did not respond after they had duly exercised the great, old-fashioned knocker, they tried the windows on the long portico. These were also locked. After quite a scramble, they scaled the portico and found a second story window open. As soon as they gained an entrance they lighted a couple of candles and proceeded to explore.

Everything was old fashioned, dusty and musty; they had expected this. Commencing on the third floor, they thoroughly overhauled everything—opening the closets, pulling aside the rotten tapestries, looking for trap doors and even sounding the walls. These actions, however, are accounted for by the fact that both had recently read Emile Gaboriau. Emulating Monsieur Lecoq, they even descended to the basement; but this was such a complex affair that they gave it up in despair.[3]

Returning to the second floor with a couple of stools and a box they had found, they proceeded to make themselves comfortable in the cleanest room they could find. Though half a dozen candles illuminated the apartment, it still seemed dreary and desolate, and dampened their high spirits "to just the pitch," as Damon said, "for a good game of chess."

By the time an hour and a half had elapsed, they concluded their first game, and a magnificent game it had been. Pythias opened his watch and remarked, "Half past twelve and no ghost."

"The reason is the room is so smoky that the poor ghosts can't become visible," replied Damon. "Throw open the window and let some of it out."

This task accomplished, they arranged the board for another game. Just as Damon stretched forth his hand to advance the white king's pawn, he suddenly stopped with a startled expression on his face, as also did Pythias. Silently, and with questioning look, they glanced at each other, and their mutual, yet incomprehensible consternation, was apparent.

Again did he essay to advance the pawn, and again did he stop, and again did they gaze, startled, into each other's faces. The silence seemed so palpable that it pressed against them like a leaden weight. The tension on their nerves was terrible, and each strove to break it, but in vain. Then they thought of the warning George had given them. Was it possible? Could it be true? Had they been deprived of the power of speech by this

---

3. Emile Gaboriau (1835–1873) was a French mystery writer. Monsieur Lecoq was Gaboriau's crime-solving detective hero.

conscious, psychic force, which neither believed in? As in a nightmare, they longed to cry out; to break the horrible, paralyzing influence. Pythias was deathly pale, while the perspiration formed in great drops on Damon's forehead, and trickling down the bridge of his nose, fell in a minute cataract upon his clean, white tie and glossy shirt front.

For an age it seemed to them, but not more than a couple of minutes they sat staring agonized at each other. At last their intuition warned them that affairs were approaching a crisis. They knew the strain could not last much longer.

Suddenly, weird and shrill, there rose on the still night air, and was wafted in through the open window, the cry of a cat; then there was a scramble as over a fence, the sound of rocks striking against boards, and the cat's triumphant cry was changed to a yowl of pain and terror which quickly turned to a choking gurgle, and they heard the enthusiastic voice of Fred cry, "Number one!"

As a diver rising from depths of ocean feels the wondrous pleasure when he drives the vitiated air from his lungs and breathes anew the essence of life, so felt they—but for a moment. The spell was not broken. Then their consternation returned, multiplied a thousand fold. Both felt a hysterical desire to laugh, so ludicrous appeared the situation. But by the mysterious power, even this was denied, and their faces were distorted in an idiotic gibber. This so horrified them, that they quickly brought their wills to bear, and their faces resumed the expression of bewilderment.

Simultaneously a light dawned upon them. They had the power of motion left. The movement of their lips had demonstrated this. They half rose, as though to flee, when the cowardice of it shamed them, and they resumed their seats. Pythias touched a bunch of firecrackers to the candle and threw them in the middle of the room.

The crackers sputtered and whizzed, snapped and banged, filling the room with a dense cloud of smoke, which hung over them like a pall, weirdly oppressive in the terrifying silence that followed.

Then a strange sensation came over Damon. All fear of the supernatural seemed to leave him, being replaced by a wild, fierce, all absorbing desire to begin the game. In a vague sort of way, he realized that he was undergoing a reincarnation. He felt himself to be rapidly evolving into some one else, or some one else was rapidly evolving into him. His own personality disappeared and as in a dream, he found another and more powerful personality had been projected into, or had overcome—swallowed up his own. To himself he seemed to have become old and feeble, as he bent under a weight of years; yet, he felt the burden to be strangely light, as though upheld by the burning, enthusiastic excitement, which boiled and bubbled and thrilled within him. He felt as though his destiny lay in the board before him; as though his life, his soul, his all, hung in the balance of the game he was to play.

Then implacable hatred and horrid desire for revenge quickened to life within him. A thousand wrongs seemed to rise before him with vivid brightness; a thousand devils seemed urging him on to the consummation of his desire. How he hated that thing—that man who was Satan incarnate, who opposed him across the chessboard. He cast a defiant glance at him, and with the swiftness of a soaring eagle, his hatred increased as he looked on the treacherous, smiling face and into the half-veiled, deceitful eyes. It was not Pythias; he was gone—why and when he did not even wonder.

As these strange things had happened to Damon, so happened they to Pythias. He despised the opponent who faced him. He felt endowed with all the cunning and low trickery of the world. The other was within his power; he knew that and was glad, as he smiled into his face with exasperating elation. The exultation to overthrow, to cast him down, rose paramount. He also desired to begin.

The game commenced. Damon boldly opened by offering the gambit. Pythias responded, but played on the defensive. Damon's attack was brilliant and rapid; but he was met by combinations so bold and novel, that by the twenty-seventh move it was broken up and Pythias still retained the gambit pawn.

Exerting himself anew, Damon, by a most sound and enduring method of attack, so placed Pythias that he had either to lose his queen or suffer mate in four moves. But by a startling series of daring moves, Pythias extricated himself with the loss of two pawns and a knight.

Elated by success, Damon attacked wildly, but was repulsed by the more cautious play of his opponent, who, by creating a diversion on the right flank, and by delicate maneuvering recovered himself, and once more grappled his adversary on equal ground. And so the game, one of the greatest the world had ever seen, proceeded. It was a mighty duel in which the participants forgot that the world still moved on, and when the first gray of dawn appeared at the window, it found Damon in a serious predicament.

He would be forced to double his rooks to avoid checkmate—he saw that. Then his opponent would check his queen under cover, and capture his red bishop. Checkmate would then be inevitable. Suddenly, however, a light broke upon the situation. A brilliant move was apparent to him. By a series of moves which he would inaugurate, he could force his adversary's queen and turn the tables.

Fate intervened. The shrill cry of a cat rose on the air and distracted his concentration. The contemplated move was lost to him, and the threatened mate so veiled the position to his reason, that he doubled his rooks, and inevitable mate in six moves confronted him.

His brain reeled; all the wrongs of a life-time hideously clamored for vengeance; all the deceits, the lies, the betrayals of his opponent, rose to his brain in startling brightness. He cursed the smiling fiend opposite him, and staggered to his feet. Murder ranged like a burning demon through his thoughts, and springing upon Pythias with an awful cry, he buried both hands in his throat. He threw him, back down, upon the chess board, and not with the rage of a fiend, but with a wonderfully sublime joy, choked him till his face grew black and agonized.

It would have gone very bad for Pythias had not a rush of feet been heard on the stairs, a couple of policemen dashed in, and with Fred and George, tore them apart.

Then Damon came, bewildered, to his senses, and helped to restore his chum.

*   *   *   *   *   *   *

"It was the old Birchall-Duinsmore murder, nearly enacted over again," said the sergeant, as they stood on the corner talking it over. "Duinsmore, his nephew, had been his life's curse. From boyhood he had always brought him trouble. As a man, he broke Birchall's heart a dozen different ways, and at last, by cunning, thievish financiering, he robbed him of all he had, except the mansion. One night, he prevailed upon the old man to stake it on a game of chess. It was all that stood between him and the potter's field, and when he lost it, he became demented, and throttled his nephew across the very board on which had been played the decisive game."

"Good chess players?"

"It has been said that they were about the best the world has ever seen."

This story was first published in the Oakland High School Aegis *on October 21, 1895 where Jack London (1876–1916) was in his senior year. The original title of this story was said to have been "A Ghostly Duel" but it was changed to the less descriptive "Who Believes in Ghosts!"*

This piece is the only one in this collection that does not specifically mention San Francisco as the locale. However, the fact that London was born in San Francisco, the reference to a "Chinese devil"—the City had the largest Chinese population in the West—and the fact that there were three separate Birchall residences there in 1895, led me to conclude that the setting was indeed San Francisco.

Over an Absinthe Bottle

by William C. Morrow

Arthur Kimberlin, a young man of very high spirit,
found himself a total stranger in San Francisco one
rainy evening, a time when his heart was breaking; for
his hunger was of that most poignant kind in which
physical suffering is forced to the highest point without
impairment of the mental functions. There remained in
his possession not a thing that he might have pawned
for a morsel to eat; and even as it was, he had stripped
his body of all articles of clothing except those which a
remaining sense of decency compelled him to retain.
Hence it was that cold assailed him and conspired with
hunger to complete his misery. Having been brought
into the world and reared a gentleman, he lacked the
courage to beg and the skill to steal. Had not an extraordinary thing occurred to him, he either would have
drowned himself in the bay within twenty-four hours or
died of pneumonia in the street.

He had been seventy hours without food, and his
mental desperation had driven him far in its race with
his physical needs to consume the strength within him;
so that now, pale, weak, and tottering, he took what
comfort he could find in the savory odors which came
steaming up from the basement kitchens of the
restaurants in Market Street, caring more to gain
them than to avoid the rain. His teeth chattered; he
shambled, stooped, and gasped. He was too desperate to
curse his fate—he could only long for food. He could not
reason; he could not understand that ten thousand
hands might gladly have fed him; he could think only of
the hunger which consumed him, and of food that could
give him warmth and happiness.

When he had arrived at Mason Street, he saw a restaurant a little way up that thoroughfare, and for that he headed, crossing the street diagonally. He stopped before the window and ogled the steaks, thick and lined with fat; big oysters lying on ice; slices of ham as large as his hat; whole roasted chickens, brown and juicy. He ground his teeth, groaned, and staggered on.

A few steps beyond was a drinking-saloon, which had a private door at one side, with the words "Family Entrance" painted thereon. In the recess of the door (which was closed) stood a man. In spite of his agony, Kimberlin saw something in this man's face that appalled and fascinated him. Night was on, and the light in the vicinity was dim; but it was apparent that the stranger had an appearance of whose character he himself must have been ignorant. Perhaps it was the unspeakable anguish of it that struck through Kimberlin's sympathies. The young man came to an uncertain halt and stared at the stranger. At first he was unseen, for the stranger looked straight out into the street with singular fixity, and the death-like pallor of his face added a weirdness to the immobility of his gaze. Then he took notice of the young man.

"Ah," he said, slowly and with peculiar distinctness, "the rain has caught you, too, without overcoat or umbrella! Stand in this doorway—there is room for two."

The voice was not unkind, though it had an alarming hardness. It was the first word that had been addressed to the sufferer since hunger had seized him, and to be spoken to at all, and have his comfort regarded in the slightest way, gave him cheer. He entered the embrasure and stood beside the stranger, who at once relapsed into his fixed gaze at nothing across the street. But presently the stranger stirred himself again.

"It may rain a long time," said he; "I am cold, and I observe that you tremble. Let us step inside and get a drink."

He opened the door and Kimberlin followed, hope beginning to lay a warm hand upon his heart. The pale stranger led the way into one of the little private booths with which the place was furnished. Before sitting down he put his hand into his pocket and drew forth a roll of bank-bills.

"You are younger than I," he said; "won't you go to the bar and buy a bottle of absinthe, and bring a pitcher of water and some glasses? I don't like for the waiters to come around. Here is a twenty-dollar bill."

Kimberlin took the bill and started down through the corridor towards the bar. He clutched the money tightly in his palm; it felt warm and comfortable, and sent a delicious tingling through his arm. How many glorious hot meals did that bill represent? He clutched it tighter and hesitated. He thought he smelled a broiled steak, with fat little mushrooms and melted butter in the steaming dish. He stopped and looked back towards the door of the booth. He saw that the stranger had closed it. He could pass it, slip out the door, and buy something to eat. He turned and started, but the coward in him (there are other names for this) tripped his resolution; so he went straight to the bar and made the purchase. This was so unusual that the man who served him looked sharply at him.

"Ain't goin' to drink all o' that, are you?" he asked.

"I have friends in the box," replied Kimberlin, "and we want to drink quietly and without interruption. We are in Number 7."

"Oh, beg pardon. That's all right," said the man.

Kimberlin's step was very much stronger and steadier as he returned with the liquor. He opened the door of the booth. The stranger sat at the side of the little table, staring at the opposite wall just as he had stared across the street. He wore a wide-brimmed, slouch hat, drawn well down. It was only after Kimberlin had set the bottle, pitcher, and glasses on the table, and seated himself opposite the stranger and within his range of vision, that the pale man noticed him.

"Oh! you have brought it? How kind of you! Now please lock the door."

Kimberlin had slipped the change into his pocket, and was in the act of bringing it out when the stranger said,—

"Keep the change. You will need it, for I am going to get it back in a way that may interest you. Let us first drink, and then I will explain."

The pale man mixed two drinks of absinthe and water, and the two drank. Kimberlin, unsophisticated, had never tasted the liquor before, and he found it harsh and offensive; but no sooner had it reached his stomach than it began to warm him, and sent the most delicious thrill through his frame.

"It will do us good," said the stranger; "presently we shall have more. Meanwhile, do you know how to throw dice?"

Kimberlin weakly confessed that he did not.

"I thought not. Well, please go to the bar and bring a dice-box. I would ring for it, but I don't want the waiters to be coming in."

Kimberlin fetched the box, again locked the door, and the game began. It was not one of the simple old games, but had complications, in which judgment, as well as chance, played a part. After a game or two without stakes, the stranger said,—

"You now seem to understand it. Very well—I will show you that you do not. We will now throw for a dollar a game, and in that way I shall win the money that you received in change. Otherwise I should be robbing you,

and I imagine you cannot afford to lose. I mean no
offence. I am a plain-spoken man, but I believe in honesty before politeness. I merely want a little diversion,
and you are so kind-natured that I am sure you will not
object."

"On the contrary," replied Kimberlin, "I shall enjoy it."

"Very well; but let us have another drink before we
start. I believe I am growing colder."

They drank again, and this time the starving man
took his liquor with relish—at least, it was something in
his stomach, and it warmed and delighted him.

The stake was a dollar a side. Kimberlin won. The
pale stranger smiled grimly, and opened another game.
Again Kimberlin won. Then the stranger pushed back
his hat and fixed that still gaze upon his opponent, smiling yet. With this full view of the pale stranger's face,
Kimberlin was more appalled than ever. He had begun
to acquire a certain self-possession and ease, and his
marveling at the singular character of the adventure had
begun to weaken, when this new incident threw him
back into confusion. It was the extraordinary expression
of the stranger's face that alarmed him. Never upon the
face of a living being had he seen a pallor so death-like
and chilling. The face was more than pale; it was white.
Kimberlin's observing faculty had been sharpened by
the absinthe, and, after having detected the stranger in
an absent-minded effort two or three times to stroke a
beard which had no existence, he reflected that some of
the whiteness of the face might be due to the recent
removal of a full beard. Besides the pallor, there were
deep and sharp lines upon the face, which the electric
light brought out very distinctly. With the exception of
the steady glance of the eyes and an occasional hard
smile, that seemed out of place upon such a face, the
expression was that of a stone inartistically cut. The
eyes were black, but of heavy expression; the lower lip

was purple; the hands were fine, white, and thin, and dark veins bulged out upon them. The stranger pulled down his hat.

"You are lucky," he said. "Suppose we try another drink. There is nothing like absinthe to sharpen one's wits, and I see that you and I are going to have a delightful game."

After the drink the game proceeded. Kimberlin won from the very first, rarely losing a game. He became greatly excited. His eyes shone; color came to his cheeks. The stranger, having exhausted the roll of bills which he first produced, drew forth another, much larger and of higher denominations. There were several thousand dollars in the roll. At Kimberlin's right hand were his winnings,—something like two hundred dollars. The stakes were raised, and the game went rapidly on. Another drink was taken. Then fortune turned the stranger's way, and he won easily. It went back to Kimberlin, for he was now playing with all the judgment and skill he could command. Once only did it occur to him to wonder what he should do with the money if he should quit winner; but a sense of honor decided him that it would belong to the stranger.

By this time the absinthe had so sharpened Kimberlin's faculties that, the temporary satisfaction which it had brought to his hunger having passed, his physical suffering returned with increased aggressiveness. Could he not order a supper with his earnings? No; that was out of the question, and the stranger said nothing about eating. Kimberlin continued to play, while the manifestations of hunger took the form of sharp pains, which darted through him viciously, causing him to writhe and grind his teeth. The stranger paid no attention, for he was now wholly absorbed in the game. He seemed puzzled and disconcerted. He played with great care, studying each throw minutely. No conversation passed between them now. They drank occasionally, the dice continued to rattle, the money kept piling up at Kimberlin's hand.

The pale man began to behave strangely. At times he would start and throw back his head, as though he were listening. For a moment his eyes would sharpen and flash, and then sink into heaviness again. More than once Kimberlin, who had now begun to suspect that his antagonist was some kind of monster, saw a frightfully ghastly expression sweep over his face, and his features would become fixed for a very short time in a peculiar grimace. It was noticeable, however, that he was steadily sinking deeper and deeper into a condition of apathy. Occasionally he would raise his eyes to Kimberlin's face after the young man had made an astonishingly lucky throw, and keep them fixed there with a steadiness that made the young man quail.

The stranger produced another roll of bills when the second was gone, and this had a value many times as great as the others together. The stakes were raised to a thousand dollars a game, and still Kimberlin won. At last the time came when the stranger braced himself for a final effort. With speech somewhat thick, but very deliberate and quiet, he said,—

"You have won seventy-four thousand dollars, which is exactly the amount I have remaining. We have been playing for several hours. I am tired, and I suppose you are. Let us finish the game. Each will now stake his all and throw a final game for it."

Without hesitation, Kimberlin agreed. The bills made a considerable pile on the table. Kimberlin threw, and the box held but one combination that could possibly beat him; this combination might be thrown once in ten thousand times. The starving man's heart beat violently as the stranger picked up the box with exasperating deliberation. It was a long time before he threw. He made his combinations and ended by defeating his opponent. He sat looking at the dice a long time, and then he slowly leaned back in his chair, settled himself comfortably, raised his eyes to Kimberlin's, and fixed that unearthly stare upon him. He said not a word; his face contained not a trace of emotion or intelligence. He simply looked. One cannot keep one's eyes open very long without winking, but the stranger did. He sat so motionless that Kimberlin began to be tortured.

"I will go now," he said to the stranger—said that when he had not a cent and was starving.

The stranger made no reply, but did not relax his gaze; and under that gaze the young man shrank back in his own chair, terrified. He became aware that two men were cautiously talking in an adjoining booth. As there was now a deathly silence in his own, he listened, and this is what he heard:

"Yes; he was seen to turn into this street about three hours ago."

"And he had shaved?"

"He must have done so; and to remove a full beard would naturally make a great change in a man."

"But it may not have been he."

"True enough; but his extreme pallor attracted attention. You know that he has been troubled with heart-disease lately, and it has affected him seriously."

"Yes, but his old skill remains. Why, this is the most daring bank-robbery we ever had here. A hundred and forty-eight thousand dollars—think of it! How long has it been since he was let out of Joliet?"

"Eight years. In that time he has grown a beard, and lived by dice-throwing with men who thought they could detect him if he should swindle them; but that is impossible. No human being can come winner out of a game with him. He is evidently not here; let us look farther."

Then the two men clinked glasses and passed out.

The dice-players—the pale one and the starving one—sat gazing at each other, with a hundred and forty-eight thousand dollars piled up between them. The winner made no move to take in the money; he merely sat and stared at Kimberlin, wholly unmoved by the conversation in the adjoining room. His imperturbability was amazing, his absolute stillness terrifying.

Kimberlin began to shake with an ague. The cold, steady gaze of the stranger sent ice into his marrow. Unable to bear longer this unwavering look, Kimberlin moved to one side, and then he was amazed to discover that the eyes of the pale man, instead of following him, remained fixed upon the spot where he had sat, or, rather, upon the wall behind it. A great dread beset the young man. He feared to make the slightest sound. Voices of men in the bar-room were audible, and the sufferer imagined that he heard others whispering and tiptoeing in the passage outside his booth. He poured out some absinthe, watching his strange companion all the while, and drank alone and unnoticed. He took a heavy drink, and it had a peculiar effect upon him: he felt his heart bounding with alarming force and rapidity and breathing was difficult. Still his hunger remained, and that and the absinthe gave him an idea that the gastric acids were destroying him by digesting his stomach. He leaned forward and whispered to the stranger, but was given no attention. One of the man's hands lay upon the table; Kimberlin placed his upon it, and then drew back in terror—the hand was as cold as a stone.

The money must not lie there exposed. Kimberlin arranged it into neat parcels, looking furtively every moment at his immovable companion, and *in mortal fear that he would stir!* Then he sat back and waited. A deadly fascination impelled him to move back into his former position, so as to bring his face directly before the gaze of the stranger. And so the two sat and stared at each other.

Kimberlin felt his breath coming heavier and his heart-beats growing weaker, but these conditions gave him comfort by reducing his anxiety and softening the pangs of hunger. He was growing more and more comfortable and yawned. If he had dared he might have gone to sleep. Suddenly a fierce light flooded his vision and sent him with a bound to his feet. Had he been struck upon the head or stabbed to the heart? No; he was sound and alive. The pale stranger still sat there staring at nothing and immovable; but Kimberlin was no longer afraid of him. On the contrary, an extraordinary buoyancy of spirit and elasticity of body made him feel reckless and daring. His former timidity and scruples vanished, and he felt equal to any adventure. Without hesitation he gathered up the money and bestowed it in his several pockets.

"I am a fool to starve," said he to himself, "with all this money ready to my hand."

As cautiously as a thief he unlocked the door, stepped out, reclosed it, and boldly and with head erect stalked out upon the street. Much to his astonishment, he found the city in the bustle of the early evening, yet the sky was clear. It was evident to him that he had not been in the saloon as long as he had supposed. He walked along the street with the utmost unconcern of the dangers that beset him, and laughed softly but gleefully. Would he not eat now—ah, would he not? Why, he could buy a dozen restaurants! Not only that, but he would hunt the city up and down for hungry men and feed them with the fattest steaks, the juiciest roasts, and the biggest oysters that the town could supply. As for himself, he must eat first; after that he would set up a great establishment for feeding other hungry mortals without charge. Yes, he would eat first; if he pleased, he

would eat till he should burst. In what single place
could he find sufficient to satisfy his hunger? Could he
live sufficiently long to have an ox killed and roasted
whole for his supper? Besides an ox he would order two
dozen broiled chickens, fifty dozen oysters, a dozen
crabs, ten dozen eggs, ten hams, eight young pigs,
twenty wild ducks, fifteen fish of four different kinds,
eight salads, four dozen bottles each of claret, bur-
gundy, and champagne; for pastry, eight plum pud-
dings, and for dessert, bushels of nuts, ices, and
confections. It would require time to prepare such a
meal, and if he could only live until it could be made
ready it would be infinitely better than to spoil his appe-
tite with a dozen or two meals of ordinary size. He
thought he could live that long, for he felt amazingly
strong and bright. Never in his life before had he walked
with so great ease and lightness; his feet hardly touched
the ground—he ran and leaped. It did him good to tan-
talize his hunger, for that would make his relish of the
feast all the keener. Oh, but how they would stare when
he would give his order, and how comically they would
hang back, and how amazed they would be when he
would throw a few thousands of dollars on the counter
and tell them to take their money out of it and keep the
change! Really, it was worthwhile to be so hungry as
that, for then eating became an unspeakable luxury.
And one must not be in too great a hurry to eat when
one is so hungry—that is beastly. How much of the joy
of living do rich people miss from eating before they are
hungry—before they have gone three days and nights
without food! And how manly it is, and how great
self-control it shows, to dally with starvation when one
has a dazzling fortune in one's pocket and every restaurant has an open door! To be hungry without money—
that is despair; to be starving with a bursting pocket—
that is sublime! Surely the only true heaven is that in

which one famishes in the presence of abundant food, which he might have for the taking, and then a gorged stomach and a long sleep!

The starving wretch, speculating thus, still kept from food. He felt himself growing in stature, and the people whom he met became pygmies. The streets widened, the stars became suns and dimmed the electric lights, and the most intoxicating odors and the sweetest music filled the air. Shouting, laughing, and singing, Kimberlin joined in a great chorus that swept over the city, and then—

The two detectives who had traced the famous bank-robber to the saloon in Mason Street, where Kimberlin had encountered the stranger of the pallid face, left the saloon; but unable to pursue the trail farther had finally returned. They found the door of booth No. 7 locked. After rapping and calling and receiving no answer, they burst open the door, and there they saw two men—one of middle age and the other very young—sitting perfectly still, and in the strangest manner imaginable staring at each other across the table. Between them was a great pile of money, arranged neatly in parcels. Near at hand were an empty absinthe bottle, a water-pitcher, glasses, and a dice-box, with the dice lying before the elder man as he had thrown them last. One of the detectives covered the elder man with a revolver and commanded,—

"Throw up your hands!"

But the dice-thrower paid no attention. The detectives exchanged startled glances. They looked closer into the faces of the two men, and then they discovered that both were dead.

Reprinted from the book The Ape, The Idiot, and Other People, *Philadelphia: J. B. Lippincott Co., 1897.*

When "Over An Absinthe Bottle" was first published on January 2, 1893 in The Argonaut *the title was "The Pale Dice-Thrower" and the younger man's name was Joseph Carringer. Four years later, when the story was reprinted (and slightly revised) in the book* The Ape, The Idiot, and Other People, *the title was changed to "Over An Absinthe Bottle" and the name Joseph Carringer became Arthur Kimberlin.*

Humorous Ghost Stories

Not all ghost stories are meant to provide chills. Here two authors have written stories that poke fun at the notion of ghosts being sinister forces.

Amy M. Parish (dates unknown) sets her story "The Ghost of Fan-Tai" in a Chinese cemetery in the Richmond District. The "ghost" turns out to be not what it was first believed to be.

Gelett Burgess (1866–1951) gives his imagination free rein in his story "The Ghost Extinguisher," which starts in San Francisco then freewheels over to Europe and then back to the U.S. You might think of his protagonist as being the first ghost buster.

Burgess lived on Russian Hill as a young man. He was founder and editor of *The Lark*, a San Francisco literary magazine that had a brief run in the mid-1890s. He was most noted for his poem "The Purple Cow":

> I never saw a Purple Cow
> I never hope to see one
> But I can tell you anyhow
> I'd rather see than be one.

"The Ghost Extinguisher" captures some of his playfulness in prose.

The Ghost of Fan-Tai

by Amy M. Parish

"Where's E Flat? Late again? Huh! Why can't that fellow be on time?" growled Haussman, leader of the Sunset Brass Band, an organization of much importance to the residents of San Francisco's new suburb and to Haussman, doing duty on all occasions, from Republican rallies, under the auspices of local Dirigos,[1] to funerals and Sunday picnics.

"Taylor, you mean?" bellowed Bauer of the bass drum. As a result of long association, Bauer's voice could almost do the work of his instrument.

"Yes, where's Taylor?" snapped Haussman. "He'll get fired, that's what he'll get—late every night."

"Well," finished Bauer, "I guess he fired himself already. Carpi told me. He had a fight mit a ghost, and the ghost fellow—vat you call it?—did him out."

"That's straight," said Carpi, who was diligently polishing his big horn.

"You know, Taylor's just bought him a little place over in the Richmond District. It's one of those affairs where the other fellow builds the house and you pay rent, just the same, with the difference that by the time you are gray, or thereabouts, you are that many dollars out; but you get the papers, all right."[2]

---

1. Dirigos appears to mean leaders or directors, from the Latin *dirigere,* meaning to direct or straighten.
2. Real estate developers known as homestead associations bought large blocks of land and built houses on speculation on them. Buyers made payments in installments until they had paid enough to receive title.

"You can get over here to Sunset in the cars for a nickel but it's a long way round, and takes all night to make the transfers; besides, when a man's paying for a home on lineman's wages, a nickel looks mighty big."

"Cut that out now, Carpi. Give us the ghost," interrupted Haussman.

"All right. I'm just telling you what Taylor's wife told my wife's sister-in-law.

"You see, to save those two nickels and the time, too, Taylor's walking over here every Saturday night. Not much of a walk, when you take the bee-line over the hill, but look at the graveyards—three of them. I'll be hanged if I'd do it to save twenty nickels and all the time there is.

"And Taylor caught it, all right. I'll bet he didn't tell his wife how scared he was, but she said he was clean out of his senses when he got home Saturday night two weeks ago.

"It was past midnight. We had practiced pretty late for that district rally, you know. The sky, I remember, was some overcast, and the wind a bit gusty. Just off the main drive in the cemetery Taylor struck west, then over a fence, cutting across a corner of the Chinese burial ground.[3]

"There was a little moon, just enough to make the shadows good and spooky! Taylor said; but he's a pretty cool chap—has to be in his work, and he'd got used to his midnight walk and wasn't a bit scary.

"Suddenly he was conscious of a sound, like a long-drawn sighing, above him, all around him. Run?

---

3. The Chinese burial ground brings to mind Lone Mountain Cemetery in the Richmond District, which had a Chinese section. The bodies were removed in the 1930s. The area today is part of the campus of the University of San Francisco.

No, you bet he didn't. He just couldn't run. No banshee
ever wailed more horribly than the next sound. As that
ceased, Taylor said he could hear the thud of his own
heart-beats. Then came another screeching, howling
and wailing, followed by the awful, inevitable rattling of
dry bones.

"In the midst of the tombs and headstones, white in
the flickering moonlight, the ghostly branches of the
eucalyptus trees writhed and slapped in the wind. Gradually, conscious that the sounds had ceased, life and
motion returned, and like a deer, by leaps and bounds,
he covered the remaining stretch of graveyard, the echo
of that banshee's wail following him as he dropped over
the wall into the street."

"Where's your fight? Is that what you call a
knock-out?"

"Hold on, Haussman," said Carpi, "my story's not
done yet. Maybe you don't know Taylor as well as I do,
but you know he's good North-Country Irish, and you
bet that break-down rankled.

"Two days later he laid off a half day, without telling
his wife, either, and made for that graveyard. There were
the tombs, big and little, the white-fenced enclosures of
long-forgotten San Francisco dead, headstones large
and small, all familiar, peaceful and quiet enough, in the
daylight. There was something else, too. Over the fence,
in the Chinese plot, a band of hired mourners were
making the day hideous with their perfunctory weeping,
while the august body of Fan-Tai, big man of the Six
Companies,[4] was being laid away for the few years the
law requires before his bones could be shipped back to

---

4. The Six Companies was—and still is—a Chinese quasi-
   governmental organization that serves the interests of
   Chinatown and its residents.

the home of his grandfathers. Here and there, moving from grave to grave, were silk-robed Celestials, placing at head and foot, among punks and tapers, foods and dainties, to pacify the devils that might seek to disturb the slumbers of their clansman.

"Taylor waited to see the friends of the gorgeous Fan-Tai depart, leaving for the feasting of his particular devils dried shad's roe, pork in its various Mongol guises, chickens prepared in every possible way, and a cunningly ornamented suckling pig.

"As the odors were carried on the wind to Taylor, concealed behind some shrubs, he decided that this was the place to stalk his ghost.

"The next Saturday night we got through here early. Well, I only wish Taylor had told us fellows—that's my quarrel with him. It would have been a lark for us all, and a darned sight better for him.

"Sure enough, when he got near that bit of fence where his path took him across the Chinese ground, the experience of the Saturday night before was repeated. First the long-drawn sighing, all about him, then wailing and howling. Taylor stopped short again, but not in fear of ghosts.

"Just in front of him stood a clump of three big eucalyptus trees, all about him the tombs and head-stones. As before, the sounds died away in an unearthly wail. Then everything was still.

"Here was where his grit had failed him before. Up in the branches of the foremost tree was a slowly moving patch of something white. The sounds began again, but Taylor stood his ground, his eyes never leaving that tree. As the wailing died away, he moved up to within twenty feet of the overhanging branches. Leveling his Smith & Wesson at that moving spot, he called out:

"'Quit your monkeying now. I'm onto your game. Come down out of there.' In an instant, the revolver was seized, and he was struggling in the arms of some one who had sprung upon him from behind a tomb. For a moment, overwhelmed by this unexpected attack and a beastly blow on the face with the butt of his own weapon, Taylor lost his head. The odds were against him all right, for he was outnumbered as well as outwitted.

"But luck favored him, and an upper-cut that would have done credit to Jim Jeffries, staggered his assailant, and then Taylor had him down and yelling for mercy. In the scuffle the revolver had been dropped, but it was within reach, and with it in his hand Taylor won out, for the fellow in the tree, now that his pal was down, and Taylor had the gun, made off, followed by two shots which hurried his steps considerably.

"Taylor was pretty well done up himself, and covered with blood from the cut which had laid his cheek open and knocked out two of his teeth, but he was able to march his prisoner over to the Park Police Station.

"While he was getting fixed up a bit, before going home, he heard the old hobo tell the sergeant that for weeks, with his pal, he had been living on devil's grub, the devotional offerings in behalf of departed moon-eyed Celestials, sleeping by night in the shelter of the tombs, well-content with Chinese food to nourish and Chinese gin to warm them. And as Taylor had suspected, to preserve the lay-out from others of their own clan, and to prevent their discovery by any chance wayfarer, they had arranged their ghostly performance.

"The police afterward found in and about that bunch of eucalyptus trees outfit enough to impersonate a whole graveyard of spooks."

"Good boy, Taylor," shouted the bandmen. "Three cheers for the E Flat!"

"Well, I'm darned," said Haussman. "But with two teeth knocked out there'll be no more cornet for him for awhile.

"Now, then, to work, boys—One, two, three, ready!"

Reprinted from the Overland Monthly, *March 1904.*

The Ghost Extinguisher

by Gelett Burgess

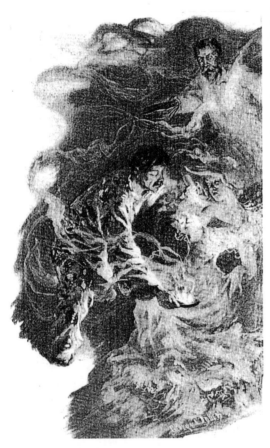

My attention was first called to the possibility of manufacturing a practicable ghost-extinguisher by a real estate agent in San Francisco.

"There's one thing," he said, "that affects city property here in a curious way. You know we have a good many murders, and, as a consequence, certain houses attain a very sensational and undesirable reputation. These houses it is almost impossible to let; you can scarcely get a decent family to occupy them rent-free. Then we have a great many places said to be haunted. These were dead timber on my hands until I happened to notice that the Japanese have no objections to spooks. Now, whenever I have such a building to rent, I let it to Japs at a nominal figure, and after they've taken the curse off, I raise the rent, the Japs move out, the place is renovated, and in the market again."

The subject interested me, for I am not only a scientist, but a speculative philosopher as well. The investigation of those phenomena that lie upon the threshold of the great unknown has always been my favorite field of research. I believed, even then, that the Oriental mind, working along different lines than those which we pursue, has attained knowledge that we know little of. Thinking, therefore, that these Japs might have some secret inherited from their misty past, I examined into the matter.

I shall not trouble you with a narration of the incidents which led up to my acquaintance with Hoku Yamanochi. Suffice it to say that I found in him a friend who was willing to share with me his whole lore of quasi-science. I call it this advisedly, for science, as we Occidentals use the term, has to do only with the laws of matter and sensation; our scientific men, in fact, recognize the existence of nothing else. The Buddhistic philosophy, however, goes further.

According to its theories, the soul is sevenfold, consisting of different shells or envelopes—something like an onion—which are shed as life passes from the material to the spiritual state. The first, or lowest, of these is the corporeal body, which, after death, decays and perishes. Next comes the vital principle, which, departing from the body, dissipates itself like an odor, and is lost. Less gross than this is the astral body, which, although immaterial, yet lies near to the consistency of matter. This astral shape, released from the body at death, remains for a while in its earthly environment, still preserving more or less definitely the imprint of the form which it inhabited.

It is this relic of a past material personality, this outworn shell, that appears, when galvanized into an appearance of life, partly materialized, as a ghost. It is not the soul that returns, for the soul, which is immortal, is composed of the four higher spiritual essences that surround the ego, and are carried on into the next life. These astral bodies, therefore, fail to terrify the Buddhists, who know them only as shadows, with no real volition. The Japs, in point of fact, have learned how to exterminate them.

There is a certain powder, Hoku informed me, which, when burnt in their presence, transforms them from the rarefied, or semi-spiritual, condition to the state of matter. The ghost, so to speak, is precipitated into and becomes a material shape which can easily be disposed of. In this state it is confined and allowed to disintegrate slowly where it can cause no further annoyance.

This long-winded explanation piqued my curiosity, which was not to be satisfied until I had seen the Japanese method applied. It was not long before I had an opportunity. A particularly revolting murder having been committed in San Francisco, my friend Hoku Yamanochi applied for the house, and, after the police had finished their examination, he was permitted to occupy it for a half-year at the ridiculous price of three dollars a month. He invited me to share his quarters, which were large and luxuriously furnished.

For a week, nothing abnormal occurred. Then, one night, I was awakened by terrifying groans, followed by a blood-curdling shriek which seemed to emerge from a large closet in my room, the scene of the late atrocity. I confess that I had all the covers pulled over my head and was shivering with horror when my Japanese friend entered, wearing a pair of flowered-silk pajamas. Hearing his voice, I peeped forth, to see him smiling reassuringly.

"You some kind of very foolish fellow," he said. "I show you how to fix him!"

He took from his pocket three conical red pastils, placed them upon a saucer and lighted them. Then, holding the fuming dish in one outstretched hand, he walked to the closed door and opened it. The shrieks burst out afresh, and, as I recalled the appalling details of the scene which had occurred in this very room only five weeks ago, I shuddered at his temerity. But he was quite calm.

Soon, I saw the wraithlike form of the recent victim dart from the closet. She crawled under my bed and ran about the room, endeavoring to escape, but was pursued by Hoku, who waved his smoking plate with indefatigable patience and dexterity.

At last he had her cornered, and the specter was caught behind a curtain of odorous fumes. Slowly the figure grew more distinct, assuming the consistency of a heavy vapor, shrinking somewhat in the operation. Hoku now hurriedly turned to me.

"You hully up, bling me one pair bellows pletty quick!" he commanded.

I ran into his room and brought the bellows from his fireplace. These he pressed flat, and then carefully inserting one toe of the ghost into the nozzle and opening the handles steadily, he sucked in a portion of the unfortunate woman's anatomy, and dexterously squirted the vapor into a large jar, which had been placed in the room for the purpose. Two more operations were necessary to withdraw the fantom completely from the corner and empty it into the jar. At last the transfer was effected and the receptacle securely stoppered and sealed.

"In formeryore-time," Hoku explained to me, "old pliests sucked ghost with mouth and spit him to inside of vase with acculacy. Modern-time method more better for stomach and epiglottis."

"How long will this ghost keep?" I inquired.

"Oh, about four, five hundled years, maybe," was his reply. "Ghost now change from spilit to matter, and comes under legality of matter as usual science."

"What are you going to do with her?" I asked.

"Send her to Buddhist temple in Japan. Old pliest use her for high celemony," was the answer.

My next desire was to obtain some of Hoku Yamanochi's ghost-powder and analyze it. For a while it defied my attempts, but, after many months of patient research, I discovered that it could be produced, in all its essential qualities, by means of a fusion of formaldehyde and hypofenyltrybrompropionic acid in an electrified vacuum. With this product I began a series of interesting experiments.

As it became necessary for me to discover the habitat of ghosts in considerable numbers, I joined the American Society for Psychical Research, thus securing desirable information in regard to haunted houses. These I visited persistently, until my powder was perfected and had been proved efficacious for the capture of any ordinary house-broken fantom. For a while I contented myself with the mere sterilization of these specters, but, as I became surer of success, I began to attempt the transfer of ghosts to receptacles wherein they could be transported and studied at my leisure, classified and preserved for future reference.

Hoku's bellows I soon discarded in favor of a large-sized bicycle pump, and eventually I had constructed one of my own, of a pattern which enabled me to inhale an entire ghost at a single stroke. With this powerful instrument I was able to compress even an adult life-sized ghost into a two-quart bottle, in the neck of which a sensitive valve (patented) prevented the specter from emerging during process.

My invention was not yet, however, quite satisfactory.

While I had no trouble in securing ghosts of recent creation—spirits, that is, who were yet of almost the consistency of matter—on several of my trips abroad in search of material I found in old manor houses or ruined castles many ancient specters so ancient that they had become highly rarefied and tenuous, scarcely visible to the naked eye. Such elusive spirits are able to pass through walls and elude pursuit with ease. It became necessary for me to obtain some instrument by which their capture could be conveniently effected.

The ordinary fire-extinguisher of commerce gave me the hint as to how this problem could be solved. One of these portable hand-instruments I filled with the proper chemicals. When inverted, the ingredients were commingled in vacuo and a vast volume of gas was liberated. This was collected in the reservoir provided with a rubber tube having a nozzle at the end. The whole apparatus being strapped upon my back, I was enabled to direct a stream of powerful precipitating gas in any desired direction, the flow being under control through the agency of a small stop-cock. By means of this ghost-extinguisher I was enabled to pursue my experiments as far as I desired.

So far my investigations had been purely scientific, but before long the commercial value of my discovery began to interest me. The ruinous effects of spectral visitations upon real estate induced me to realize some pecuniary reward from my ghost-extinguisher, and I began to advertise my business. By degrees, I became known as an expert in my original line, and my professional services were sought with as much confidence as those of a veterinary surgeon. I manufactured the Gerrish Ghost-Extinguisher in several sizes, and put it on the market, following this venture with the introduction of my justly celebrated Gerrish Ghost-Grenades. These hand-implements were made to be kept in racks conveniently distributed in country houses for cases of sudden emergency. A single grenade, hurled at any spectral form, would, in breaking, liberate enough formaldybrom to coagulate the most perverse spirit, and the resulting vapor could easily be removed from the room by a housemaid with a common broom.

This branch of my business, however, never proved profitable, for the appearance of ghosts, especially in the United States, is seldom anticipated. Had it been possible for me to invent a preventive as well as a remedy, I might now be a millionaire; but there are limits even to modern science.

Having exhausted the field at home, I visited England in the hope of securing customers among the country families there. To my surprise, I discovered that the possession of a family specter was considered as a permanent improvement to the property, and my offers of service in ridding houses of ghostly tenants awakened the liveliest resentment. As a layer of ghosts I was much lower in the social scale than a layer of carpets.

Disappointed and discouraged, I returned home to make a further study of the opportunities of my invention. I had, it seemed, exhausted the possibilities of the use of unwelcome fantoms. Could I not, I thought, derive a revenue from the traffic in desirable specters? I decided to renew my investigations.

The nebulous spirits preserved in my laboratory, which I had graded and classified, were, you will remember, in a state of suspended animation. They were, virtually, embalmed apparitions, their inevitable decay delayed, rather than prevented. The assorted ghosts that I had now preserved in hermetically sealed tins were thus in a state of unstable equilibrium. The tins once opened and the vapor allowed to dissipate, the original astral body would in time be reconstructed and the warmed-over specter would continue its previous career.

But this process, when naturally performed, took years. The interval was quite too long for the fantom to be handled in any commercial way. My problem was, therefore, to produce from my tinned Essence of Ghost a specter that was capable of immediately going into business and that could haunt a house while you wait.

It was not until radium was discovered that I approached the solution of my great problem, and even then months of indefatigable labor were necessary before the process was perfected. It has now been well demonstrated that the emanations of radiant energy sent forth by this surprising element defy our former scientific conceptions of the constitution of matter. It was for me to prove that the vibratory activity of radium (whose amplitudes and intensity are undoubtedly four-dimensional) effects a sort of allotropic modification in the particles of that imponderable ether which seems to lie half-way between matter and pure spirit. This is as far as I need to go in my explanation, for a full discussion involves the use of quaternions and the method of least squares. It will be sufficient for the layman to know that my preserved fantoms, rendered radio-active, would, upon contact with the air, resume their spectral shape.

The possible extension of my business now was enormous, limited only by the difficulty in collecting the necessary stock. It was by this time almost as difficult to get ghosts as it was to get radium. Finding that a part of my stock had spoiled, I was now possessed of only a few dozen cans of apparitions, many of these being of inferior quality. I immediately set about replenishing my raw material. It was not enough for me to pick up a ghost here and there, as one might get old mahogany; I determined to procure my fantoms in wholesale lots.

Accident favored my design. In an old volume of "Blackwood's Magazine" I happened, one day, to come across an interesting article upon the battle of Waterloo. It mentioned, incidentally, a legend to the effect that every year, upon the anniversary of the celebrated victory, spectral squadrons had been seen by the peasants charging battalions of ghostly grenadiers. Here was my opportunity.

I made elaborate preparations for the capture of this job-lot of fantoms upon the next anniversary of the fight. Hard by the fatal ditch which engulfed Napoleon's cavalry I stationed a corps of able assistants provided with rapid-fire extinguishers ready to enfilade the famous sunken road. I stationed myself with a No. 4 model magazine-hose, with a four-inch nozzle, directly in the path which I knew would be taken by the advancing squadron.

It was a fine, clear night, lighted, at first, by a slice of new moon; but later, dark, except for the pale illumination of the stars. I have seen many ghosts in my time—ghosts in garden and garret, at noon, at dusk, at dawn, fantoms fanciful, and specters sad and spectacular—but never have I seen such an impressive sight as this nocturnal charge of cuirassiers, galloping in goblin glory to their time-honored doom. From afar the French reserves presented the appearance of a nebulous mass, like a low-lying cloud or fog-bank, faintly luminous, shot with fluorescent gleams. As the squadron drew nearer in its desperate charge, the separate forms of the troopers shaped themselves, and the galloping guardsmen grew ghastly with supernatural splendor.

Although I knew them to be immaterial and without mass or weight, I was terrified at their approach, fearing to be swept under the hoofs of the nightmares they rode. Like one in a dream, I started to run, but in another instant they were upon me, and I turned on my stream of formaldybrom. Then I was overwhelmed in a cloud-burst of wild warlike wraiths.

The column swept past me, over the bank, plunging to its historic fate. The cut was piled full of frenzied, scrambling specters, as rank after rank swept down into the horrid gut. At last the ditch swarmed full of writhing forms and the carnage was dire.

My assistants with the extinguishers stood firm, and although almost unnerved by the sight, they summoned their courage, and directed simultaneous streams of formaldybrom into the struggling mass of fantoms. As soon as my mind returned, I busied myself with the huge tanks I had prepared for use as receivers. These were fitted with a mechanism similar to that employed in portable forges, by which the heavy vapor was sucked off. Luckily the night was calm, and I was enabled to fill a dozen cylinders with the precipitated ghosts. The segregation of individual forms was, of course, impossible, so that men and horses were mingled in a horrible mixture of fricasseed spirits. I intended subsequently to empty the soup into a large reservoir and allow the separate specters to re-form according to the laws of spiritual cohesion.

Circumstances, however, prevented my ever accomplishing this result. I returned home, to find awaiting me an order so large and important that I had no time in which to operate upon my cylinders of cavalry.

My patron was the proprietor of a new sanatorium for nervous invalids, located near some medicinal springs in the Catskills. His building was unfortunately located, having been built upon the site of a once-famous summer-hotel, which, while filled with guests, had burnt to the ground, scores of lives having been lost. Just before the patients were to be installed in the new structure, it was found that the place was haunted by the victims of the conflagration to a degree that rendered it inconvenient as a health-resort. My professional services were requested, therefore, to render the building a fitting abode for convalescents. I wrote to the proprietor, fixing my charge at five thousand dollars. As my usual rate was one hundred dollars per ghost, and over a hundred lives were lost at the fire, I considered this price reasonable, and my offer was accepted.

The sanatorium job was finished in a week. I secured one hundred and two superior spectral specimens, and upon my return to the laboratory, put them up in heavily embossed tins with attractive labels in colors.

My delight at the outcome of this business was, however, soon transformed to anger and indignation. The proprietor of the health-resort, having found that the specters from his place had been sold, claimed a rebate upon the contract price equal to the value of the modified ghosts transferred to my possession. This, of course, I could not allow. I wrote, demanding immediate payment according to our agreement, and this was peremptorily refused. The manager's letter was insulting in the extreme. The Pied Piper of Hamelin was not worse treated than I felt myself to be; so, like the piper, I determined to have my revenge.

I got out the twelve tanks of Waterloo ghost-hash from the store-rooms, and treated them with radium for two days. These I shipped to the Catskills billed as hydrogen gas. Then, accompanied by two trustworthy assistants, I went to the sanatorium and preferred my demand for payment in person. I was ejected with contumely. Before my hasty exit, however, I had the satisfaction of noticing that the building was filled with patients. Languid ladies were seated in wicker-chairs upon the piazzas, and frail anemic girls filled the corridors. It was a hospital of nervous wrecks whom the slightest disturbance would throw into a panic. I suppressed all my finer feelings of mercy and kindness and smiled grimly as I walked back to the village.

That night was black and lowering, fitting weather for the pandemonium I was about to turn loose. At ten o'clock, I loaded a wagon with the tanks of compressed cohorts, and, muffled in heavy overcoats, we drove to the sanatorium. All was silent as we approached; all was dark. The wagon concealed in a grove of pines, we took out the tanks, one by one, and placed them beneath the ground-floor windows. The sashes were easily forced open, and raised enough to enable us to insert the rubber tubes connected with the iron reservoirs. At midnight everything was ready.

I gave the word, and my assistants ran from tank to tank, opening the stop-cocks. With a hiss as of escaping steam the huge vessels emptied themselves, vomiting forth clouds of vapor, which, upon contact with the air, coagulated into strange shapes, as the white of an egg does when dropped into boiling water. The rooms became instantly filled with dismembered shades of men and horses seeking wildly to unite themselves with their proper parts.

Legs ran down the corridors, seeking their respective trunks, arms writhed wildly reaching for missing bodies, heads rolled hither and yon in search of native necks. Horses' tails and hoofs whisked and hurried in quest of equine ownership until, reorganized, the spectral steeds galloped about to find their riders.

Had it been possible, I would have stopped this riot of wraiths long ere this, for it was more awful than I had anticipated, but it was already too late. Cowering in the garden, I began to hear the screams of awakened and distracted patients. In another moment, the front door of the hotel was burst open, and a mob of hysterical women in expensive nightgowns rushed out upon the lawn, and huddled in shrieking groups.

I fled into the night.

I fled, but Napoleon's men fled with me. Compelled by I know not what fatal astral attraction, perhaps the subtle affinity of the creature for the creator, the spectral shells, moved by some mysterious mechanics of spiritual being, pursued me with fatuous fury. I sought refuge, first, in my laboratory, but, even as I approached, a lurid glare foretold me of its destruction. As I drew nearer, the whole ghost-factory was seen to be in flames; every moment crackling reports were heard, as the overheated tins of phantasmagoria exploded and threw their supernatural contents upon the night. These liberated ghosts joined the army of Napoleon's outraged warriors, and turned upon me. There was not enough formaldybrom in all the world to quench their fierce energy. There was no place in all the world safe for me from their visitation. No ghost-extinguisher was powerful enough to lay the host of spirits that haunted me henceforth, and I had neither time nor money left with which to construct new Gatling quick-firing tanks.

It is little comfort to me to know that one hundred nervous invalids were completely restored to health by means of the terrific shock which I administered.

Reprinted from Cosmopolitan Magazine *April 1905.*

20th-Century Ghost Stories

The stories in this section differ in their approaches.

"The Vanishing Hitchhiker" is a classic American folktale that came into vogue during the 1920s as the automobile gained ascendancy. Vanishing hitchhiker stories have been set in other American cities as well as San Francisco. This rendition was part of a 1942 article in *California Folklore Quarterly* that analyzed the origins of the vanishing hitchhiker story.

"Death of a Good Cook," beautifully written by Sara Gerstle (1874–1956), daughter of a prominent San Francisco Jewish family, who tells the story of an affluent couple whose Chinese cook encounters a ghost.

In "The Phantom Still Flees," Barbara Smith recounts the story of Flora Sommerton, the runaway bride whose ghost is closely associated with the place where she is said to have disappeared—Nob Hill. In "Spirits of Alcatraz," Smith describes the convicts who served time on "The Rock" when it was a federal penitentiary, and whose ghosts still allegedly linger there today.

In "The Press Club's Ghost," written in 1964 by Press Club member Col. Carroll E. B. Peeke (1898–1991), the author tells the history of the famed Mexican bandit Joaquin Murrieta, and leaves the reader to decide whether his ghost haunted the old San Francisco Press Club. He starts his story on a teasing note with a play on the word spirits. And he ends with a question that might be asked about any ghost story or about the existence of ghosts in general: "What do YOU think?"

The Vanishing Hitchhiker

by Richard K. Beardsley and Rosalie Hankey

This is the story just as we heard it several months ago, from a level-headed, conscientious businessman. "I've never been able to understand this," he began hesitatingly. "It happened to a friend of mine, Sam Kerns, a fellow who went to Cal with me. He can't explain it either.

"Kerns and another man were driving home from a party in San Francisco. It was a wretched night, bitingly cold and raining with such violence that driving was difficult. As they drew near a stop sign on Mission Street they made out the indistinct form of a woman standing on the corner, quite alone, as if she were waiting for someone. Since it was after two o'clock in the morning and they knew that the street cars no longer were running, they stared at her curiously as they drew up to the corner. Then Kerns brought the car to a sharp halt, for standing in the pouring rain without a coat or an umbrella was a lovely girl, dressed in a thin white evening gown.

"She was evidently in some embarrassment or trouble so without hesitation they offered to take her home. She accepted and got into the back seat of their two-door sedan. Realizing that she must be chilled, they wrapped her in the car blanket. She gave them an address near Twin Peaks and added that she lived there with her mother. However, she made no attempt to explain her presence on Mission Street in the pouring rain, without coat or umbrella. The men started toward Twin Peaks making some efforts at conversation, to which the girl responded politely but in a manner which showed plainly that she did not care to talk. When they reached Fifth Street, Kern's friend looked round to see if she were comfortable. There was no one in the back seat. Startled, he leaned over to see if she might have fallen to the floor, but, except for the crumpled blanket, there was nothing to be seen. Amazed and frightened, he made Kerns stop the car. Without doubt the girl was gone.

"The only possible explanation of her disappearance was that she had slipped quietly out of the car; but they had not stopped since picking her up. That she could have jumped from the car while it was moving and closed the door behind her was almost impossible. Thoroughly puzzled and not a little worried, they decided to go to the address she had given. After some difficulty they found the house, an old ramshackle building with a dim light showing from the interior. They knocked and after long wait the door was opened by a frail old woman, clutching a shawl over her shoulders. As they began their story they were struck by the complete incredibility of the entire business. Feeling more and more foolish they stumbled on as best they could. The old woman listened patiently, almost as if she had heard the same story before. When they had finished, she smiled wanly, 'Where did you say you picked her up?' she asked. 'On First and Mission,' Kerns replied.

"'That was my daughter,' the old woman said. 'She was killed in an automobile accident at First and Mission two years ago.'"

Reprinted from California Folklore Quarterly, *Vol. I, Number 4, October 1942.*

Death of a Good Cook

by Sara Gerstle

Tung was the first cook I had when I married and set
up my own home, and one of the best I ever had in
many years of housekeeping. Only those who knew San
Francisco in the dear old, dead old days before the First
World War can understand what a joy the Chinese
cooks of that era were. They were almost always artists
in their line, and their line embraced every branch of
cookery from tournedos Henri IV to cakes and pastries
that would do credit to Rumpelmeyer.[1] Nothing was too
much trouble for them; they would spend hours carving
exquisite flowers from carrots and turnips to garnish a
meat dish, or performing minor miracles in spun sugar
to beautify an ice. No ordering ices or cakes from a
caterer in those days, when Wong or Li or Tung could
produce something far better in your own kitchen; and
as for company, they loved it, bless their hearts, for
although we were not supposed to know about that,
they quietly practiced the time-honored Chinese system
of squeeze, and the extra meat and poultry and grocer-
ies needed for a dinner party meant so much more
commission from the tradespeople for honest John
Chinaman. And if they slipped out every night as soon
as the dinner dishes were done to gamble in the mysterious dives of Chinatown, who cared? They were always
on hand, immaculate and efficient, to serve breakfast,
and if most of their wages (absurdly low by present-day

---

1. Rumpelmeyer was a celebrated Parisian confectioner who was
   active during the early- to mid-20th century.

standards) passed over the fan-tan[2] table, that was undoubtedly hard on their families, but not the employer's business.

Tung was typical in every way of this noble, and now all but extinct, race of Chinese cooks, and for all my youth and inexperience my household ran smoothly, thanks to him and to my faithful Irish Mollie, who was passionately superstitious and afraid of her own shadow, but otherwise an excellent maid. The house was brand new, bright and gay, everything was as I wanted it, and I must have been rather unsympathetic when I heard other young matrons complaining about their domestic difficulties. Until things started to happen.

One morning when I was in the kitchen discussing the day's menus with Tung, he suddenly asked:

"Missy, you ask man come fix maybe telephone, maybe 'lectric light?"

"No, I didn't. Is anything out of order?"

"No out of order, evvything fine. I see man I think maybe Missy send for."

I became vaguely uneasy.

"Where did you see a man, Tung?"

"I see um cellar, yesterday, then this morning. I think workman, come fix something. I say 'What you want?' He no answer me, I think maybe he no hear, so I say 'Who tell you come?' He no talk, then bimbe he no there."

"Was the cellar door open?"

"Cellar door closed. I look: Flont door closed, back door closed. S'pose no man ling bell, no man can come in. My no savvy how that man come in."

---

2. A gambling game especially popular among the Chinese.

I didn't savvy either, and I didn't like it, but all I could do was tell Tung to be extra careful about keeping the house securely locked, and not to tell Mollie about the man, because she was terribly timid, and I was afraid she might leave if she knew an unknown man had been prowling around the cellar. I decided to tell my husband about it when he came home that evening.

He was naturally concerned, and went straight to the kitchen to question Tung. I imagine the cook was none too pleased to be interrupted in the midst of his preparations for dinner, but he repeated what he had told me, showed where he had seen the man, and Bill returned to the living room convinced that Tung had undeniably seen a man in the cellar. But how could the man have got in? Tung had always been scrupulously careful about keeping doors closed, the doors all had spring locks, and the basement windows were barred. As my husband mixed himself a cocktail, he looked at me with an odd expression.

"Do you suppose Tung could have had—well, a sort of hallucination?" he suggested.

"I never heard of a Chinese with hallucinations," I replied. "They are intensely practical people. And if you are thinking that there is something supernatural about this, I can only say, whoever heard of a house as new as this one being haunted? No one has even had time to die in it yet."

"That's just the point. Someone did." Bill was looking self-conscious and rather avoiding my eyes.

"What on earth do you mean?"

"My dear, it was no one either of us had ever seen, as far as I know, and I didn't tell you about it at the time, for you were just beginning to expect the baby, and I was afraid of giving you a shock. But only a few weeks before we moved in, one of the workmen committed suicide—no one seemed to know why—and of course I was told about it. They found his body in the cellar, where he had been working on the electric installation."

"In the cellar?" I said, in rather a small voice.

"Yes. Oh, there's no connection, of course, and I don't really believe in such things; but I'm not sure I wouldn't prefer a nice immaterial ghost, especially if he sticks to the cellar, to a live burglar. I never heard of a ghost doing any harm either to life or property, did you?"

"N-no, I suppose not, except that they could scare the wits out of people. Mollie, for instance. She believes in everything, from banshees to leprechauns, and the unfortunate thing about superstitious people is that they never seem to get any fun out of their superstitions—they just get scared. Mollie wouldn't stay an hour in a house she thought was haunted. And she's an awfully good maid."

"She doesn't often go to the cellar, does she?"

"Hardly ever, I think. Nobody goes there except Tung and the laundress, and tradespeople."

"Then there's nothing to worry about, unless our unknown man turns up on one of the other floors; then of course we must do something about it."

"Such as?"

I wonder why it is that men always look annoyed when one asks a simple, pertinent question.

"Well, send for the police if he seems to be alive, and—er—do whatever one does about ghosts if he doesn't."

"Bill, you can't sprinkle Keating's powder[3] or get in fumigators to rid a house of ghosts, you know. It isn't that easy."

---

3. An anti-insect powder.

"You can call in a clergyman to exorcise them. I've read about it, it's most interesting. There is actually a ritual, although of course it is almost never resorted to nowadays."

I said it was the most absurd, medieval claptrap I had ever heard, and he'd be talking about witchcraft next. He said amiably that it was only a suggestion, and poured a second cocktail. Then I had another, most disquieting idea.

"But suppose the man hangs around, and Tung gets frightened and leaves? He's one of the best cooks in San Francisco; I'd have a fit if he left us."

"He doesn't seem a nervous type to me."

"Nervous, my foot! I don't think I am an especially nervous woman, but I take a very low view of an uninvited workman, dead or alive, prowling about my house. And Tung sleeps in the basement, don't forget that."

"I don't think the man killed himself anywhere near the cook's room. I think it was near the electric switchboard."

"And is it supposed to be ghost etiquette to stick to the spot where you died?" I asked sarcastically.

"How should I know? I've never been a ghost. In fact, the only ones I've ever known are Shakespeare's ghosts, and they turn up all over the place, now that I think of it."

That made me laugh, and lessened the tension, and we got down to trying to decide which was the lesser of two evils—a ghost and terrified servants, or a live intruder and a terrified me. Finally we evolved the not very satisfactory theory that Tung might have been suffering from a slight opium hangover (not that we had the faintest reason to believe he smoked, but after all it was a Chinese vice) and had really been the victim of an hallucination.

Afterward it seemed almost indecent that we should have treated the matter as lightly as we did, but to this day I have no idea whether the man Tung saw, or thought he saw, in the cellar had any connection with what happened a few days later.

I awoke one morning with a bad headache and decided to spend the day quietly in my room, as we were dining out. So when Mollie brought my breakfast tray I sent word by her to Tung that I would not come down to the kitchen as usual to discuss the day's meals with him—there would be no dinner, and all I wanted for lunch was tea and toast at one o'clock.

By lunchtime my headache had practically disappeared, but instead of the tea and toast all I got was a very pale and violently trembling Mollie, who burst into my room sobbing.

"Oh, please, ma'am, something terrible has happened –oh, I'm that scared—oh, it's awful—"

"Mollie, stop crying and tell me what is wrong. What has happened?"

She swallowed convulsively, dabbed her eyes with her organdy apron, and strove to get her voice under control.

"It's Tung, ma'am. I went to the kitchen to get the tray ready for your lunch, and Tung wasn't there, and the kettle wasn't boiling for your tea or anything. So I called down the cellar stairs and he didn't answer, so I went down to his room, and—and—oh, holy saints in Heaven, I'm afraid he's dead!"

By this time I was out of bed, wriggling into my slippers and pulling on a dressing gown.

"Come on, we'll go down and see what's the matter. Don't be frightened, probably he's just feeling faint."

Feeling faint was the last thing I would have connected with my competent, industrious, well poised Tung, but it was the only explanation I could think of at the moment, and poor Mollie was obviously in desperate need of reassurance. Together we hurried down to the kitchen, and from there to the stairway that led to the cellar. But at the head of the stairs Mollie froze into immobility.

"I can't go down, ma'am. If the Blessed Mother herself offered me a golden crown to go down to that cellar, I simply couldn't."

"Mollie, you are being very childish and silly," I scolded her. "But stay here if you want to, and I'll go down. There is absolutely nothing to be afraid of."

I murmured that last phrase over to myself, presumably because I liked the sound of it, as I descended the narrow cement stair. *Naturally* there was nothing to be afraid of. Nevertheless, I should have been just as happy if there had been someone with me.

The cellar was cool, neat and empty. On one side were the laundry, storage room and wine closet, on the other the furnace room, coal cellar, a door leading into the garage, another door to the garden, and, dead ahead, the cook's room, with its door ajar. One glance into that room, and I became as motionless as Mollie and, I grieve to admit, almost as terrified.

On the narrow iron bed lay Tung, his head rolled to one side, and even my inexperienced eyes told me that he would never speak to me again. Sitting beside him, a hand on his arm, was a man in blue denim overalls, his back to me so that I could not see his face.

One does stupid things at such a time. I had never seen a dead person, but I felt completely certain that poor Tung was dead; and yet, from force of habit I called to him:

"Tung, what has happened? Speak to me!"

My voice sounded hollow and strange in the silent place, and a strangled sob came from the head of the stairs, where Mollie was probably clutching her rosary, which I knew she always carried in her pocket, and praying that I would come to no harm. I didn't mind the idea. Prayers can't hurt.

Then I remembered the man who was sitting beside the bed, and turned to ask him what had happened, and how he came to be there. He was gone.

At that moment, for the first time in my life, I knew the meaning of sheer panic, and it took more self-control than I knew I possessed not to run screaming up the stairs or out through the door that led to the garden. I had barely sense enough to remember that that would do no good at all, and that I should be desperately ashamed of myself afterward. I set my jaw to keep my teeth from chattering, and tried to reason things out.

The cook's room was not a large one, and had only two doors, the one through which I was looking, and one opening into a clothes closet. To leave the room, the unknown man would have had either to brush past me or, if he wanted to take refuge in the closet, pass directly across my line of vision, between the bed and me. And he had done neither of those things. The only other possible means of egress, the window, was not accessible to anything larger than a cat, for being level with the garden, it was protected by closely set iron bars—besides which, even if the bars had been removed, no one could have passed through the window without my seeing him, for it was directly opposite the door.

I forced myself to inspect the closet, the bathroom next door, and the doors leading to the garage and garden. The two latter were securely closed, the bathroom and closet were empty. It took more courage than I had to carry the search to the laundry and other rooms—besides, the man couldn't possibly have reached anyone of them without passing me. Whoever came from the Coroner's office, or wherever I must telephone, I would have to complete the inspection of the cellar. I fled up the stairs, the heels of my mules making an unholy clatter on the bare steps.

That is really all the story. You can think what you like. The Coroner's verdict, stripped of its medical phraseology, boiled down to death due to heart failure. A thorough search of the basement revealed no trace of an intruder and no possible means by which one could have entered. I never knew if my poor Tung had died of fright, or if I had simply imagined the man.

In all the years she remained with us, Mollie would never consent to go to the cellar; I think she would have given notice rather than set foot in what she considered an accursed place.

On the other hand, not one of the cooks who succeeded Tung and occupied his room ever mentioned seeing anyone in the cellar except the perfectly ordinary tradesmen who came to make deliveries.

So there you are.

This story was originally published in 1951 as part of a book called Four Ghost Stories. *It was privately printed in a limited edition of 150 copies. The only public place in San Francisco that has a copy is the Rare Book Room of the Gleeson Library on the campus of the University of San Francisco.*

The book's introduction, which was written by author Sara Gerstle's daughter, Miriam, profiled her mother as a gray-haired woman who wrote these stories while recuperating in a hospital from an illness. Sara Gerstle died in New York five years after Four Ghost Stories *was published.*

The Phantom Still Flees

by Barbara Smith

World War I—the "war to end all wars"—had ended; the Great Depression had not yet begun. The Roaring Twenties were in full swing, and America had become the Promised Land where anything and everything seemed possible. Not everyone, however, was free to enjoy the prosperity. Then, as now, there were the sad few who were hostages to their pasts.

On a gray morning in 1926, the population of those unfortunate, imprisoned souls was reduced by one when the disease-ridden corpse of a 68-year old woman was discovered in Butte, Montana. Flora Sommerton had died alone in the tiny flophouse room where she had lived for as long as anyone could remember.

That same day, more than a thousand miles away, on California Street in San Francisco's Nob Hill district, a misty presence appeared—an apparition of a beautiful young woman dressed in a flowing, beaded gown. Her demeanor suggested that she was in turmoil and fleeing from someone only she could see.

It was some time before anyone made a connection between those two seemingly disparate events, but as the frightened-looking ghost began to appear more and more frequently, details about her spread throughout the community. Older folks in the area listened especially carefully to those who'd seen the ghost. Descriptions of the formally dressed, seemingly confused entity reminded them of an incident that had occurred when they were young—the social disaster of their era.

These older people could still clearly recall the year 1876 and the formal party that Mr. and Mrs. Sommerton hosted for their 18-year-old daughter, Flora. The gathering was to be the gala event of the year. Unlike many parties of this sort, Flora's was not a debutante ball. The Sommertons were not hoping to present their daughter to eligible males—far from it. They had already chosen Flora's future husband. He was the son of an equally wealthy and established family. What they hadn't taken into account, however, was Flora's dramatic reaction to their plans. She felt no affection for the man they wanted her to marry and had become deeply depressed at the thought of spending her life with him. Despite the intensity of her feelings, the young woman said nothing to discourage her parents' actions.

Therefore, the Sommertons' plans went ahead. The party was well underway and their daughter's engagement was just about to be announced when the prospective bride panicked. Still wearing her exquisite gown, Flora bolted from the house and fled down the street. A few of the party guests tried to follow her, but the desperate young woman disappeared over the crest of a hill and into thin air.

Now it was her parents' turn to panic. Flora, whom they had always protected from the realities of outside life, was somewhere out on the streets with absolutely no resources. When their daughter had still not been found the next day, Mr. Sommerton notified the authorities. Despite widespread publicity, an intensive search, and the offer of a $250,000 reward, Flora's parents never saw her again. They died heartbroken and alone, never recovering from their terrible loss.

The Sommertons had no way of knowing that their daughter was still alive and managing to scrape together a meager existence far from the pampered world in which she'd been raised. It wasn't until her death in a Montana flophouse that anyone who knew Flora Sommerton as a young woman learned that she had lived to a ripe old age despite her apparent naiveté and lack of practical life skills.

The ghost of the young, fleeing Flora wearing a formal, beaded gown continues to appear even today. She is always seen on the same street she ran along to escape the future she could not bear to face. Sadly, no one has been able to help Flora accept her fate; as a ghost, the former Miss Sommerton seems to be in a separate dimension and therefore feels no connection to today's world. Perhaps her soul passed on to another plane the very day she died and what people are seeing is just a ghostly replay of the terrible trauma Flora experienced on the night in 1876 when she disappeared from San Francisco's high society.

If you ever have the opportunity to take the cable car up Nob Hill, be extra vigilant in watching the passers-by as you approach the Fairmont Hotel. The young woman in the long gown may not be an eccentric street person —she may be the frantic ghost of Flora Sommerton.

Reprinted from Ghost Stories of California *(2000) by Barbara Smith, with the kind permission of the author and Lone Pine Publishing.*

Spirits of Alcatraz

by Barbara Smith

The remaining buildings on Alcatraz Island are, without a doubt, the coldest places I have ever personally set foot. It's probably safe to say that anyone with even an ounce of sensitivity who has visited the site will concur.

The Miwok Indians were the first people to feel uncomfortable about the severe-looking chunk of rock jutting out of the waters of San Francisco Bay. Long before concrete fortresses were constructed to house the country's most dangerous criminals, the area natives studiously avoided Alcatraz ("island of pelicans"), believing it to be evil. Given this history, it's ironic that people now eagerly pay for the privilege of visiting "the Rock."

The first real use of the frequently fog-shrouded island was as a strategic spot for a lighthouse designed to steer unsuspecting ships away from its rocky coast-lines. Five years later, in 1859, authorities decided that the isolated location would make it a formidable venue for a prison. No one, it was reasoned, could ever escape from the remote island.

As a federal penal institution, Alcatraz was intended to house only the worst and most dangerous criminals—those judged to be beyond hope of rehabilitation. This was never a facility designed to do anything but punish the inmates and keep them from posing a threat to law-abiding citizens. As a result, many of the most infamous gangsters in American history were banished to the bleak isolation of the Rock. Al Capone, "Machine Gun" Kelly, "Creepy" Karpis, "Doc" Barker ("Ma" Barker's son) and "Butcher" Maldowitz were just a few of the best known. Robert Stroud, whose study of local birds earned him the nickname "the Birdman of Alcatraz," remains the only man ever incarcerated on the island to be remembered for anything other than villainous deeds.

Many of the guards at Alcatraz became as malevolent as the inmates, probably because they, too, were effectively isolated from civilization. The staff's often horrendous cruelty to the prisoners was brought to light during an investigation into a 1946 escape attempt. From that time until the facility was decommissioned in 1963, the population of Alcatraz steadily declined—the living population, that is. Even today, the ghosts of many prisoners continue to haunt the island.

Oddly enough, it is not just the spirits of the prisoners who died while serving sentences on Alcatraz Island whose souls remain. Some of those who died elsewhere have returned to haunt the place. Most of the hauntings take the form of inexplicable sounds. People frequently hear gruesome, ghostly sounds—men screaming and crying, walking or running through the corridors, whispering to the other souls who were their fellow inmates.

One cellblock has been the site of so much ghostly activity that esteemed psychic Sylvia Brown was called in to investigate. An examination of her findings indicates the presence of Abie "Butcher" Maldowitz, an especially vicious man who was eventually killed by a fellow inmate. His disembodied soul, it would seem, is just as angry in death as the man was in life.

On D Block, Cell 14 continues to resonate with the sorrow and despair of a criminal who spent three solitary years in the tiny area. Today, no matter how warm the weather, that one cell remains icy cold.

The banjo-playing specter in the shower room is generally accepted as being the ghost of Al Capone. Yes, the notorious gangland boss whom the FBI nicknamed

"Scarface" played the banjo during his incarceration on the Rock!

Not surprisingly, the quietest spirit in the place is the ghost of Robert Stroud—the Birdman of Alcatraz. After murdering a man in Alaska, Stroud was sentenced to serve 12 years in Leavenworth penitentiary. He spent his time behind bars studying birds and became an expert ornithologist. Shortly before his release date, he killed one of the guards and was sentenced to death. President Wilson commuted the order to life in solitary confinement, keeping Stroud alive only so that he might continue to research and write about birds—and this is exactly what the prisoner did for the next 20 years. Eventually the Birdman was released from Alcatraz, but since his death in 1963 visitors to the island have been hearing Stroud's distinctive whistle attempting to reach his beloved birds from beyond the grave.

While Alcatraz is definitely a fascinating spot for ghost enthusiasts to explore, those who choose to do so would be wise to remember that all the entities in the place were hardened criminals in life. Even Stroud, perhaps the least aggressive soul ever confined on the island, was responsible for the deaths of two people. For this reason, the "island of pelicans" is not the safest haunted place for a ghost hunt.

Reprinted from Ghost Stories of California *(2000) by Barbara Smith, with the kind permission of the author and Lone Pine Publishing.*

The Press Club's Ghost

by Col. Carroll E. B. Peeke

Many members of the Club have been known—at times —to commune with spirits, particularly in the second floor bar. But there is one member—who desires to remain anonymous—who claims that he has seen, not once but several times, a ghost on the first floor.

Mr. X, as we shall refer to him, is a long-time member of the Club. Here is his story as he related it. Read it and judge for yourself if the Club has its own ghost.

"I had spent the evening on the second floor," Mr. X admitted, "and when closing time came I decided to take a walk, to get some fresh air in my lungs and clear my head.

"It was a miserable night, dense fog and a chill wind, so I made my walk a short one. As I started back to the Club, walking up Post Street, I heard footsteps following me. I looked back over my shoulder, a bit apprehensive, but the fog was so thick I could see nothing.

"I quickened my pace. So did the person following me. Finally I reached the Club and walked into the lobby. A moment later the door opened and in came a shadowy figure, faintly luminous. It resembled no one I had ever seen before, so I said sharply:

"This is a private club, for members only. What are you doing here and what do you want?

"In a muffled voice, speaking perfect English but with a Spanish accent the figure replied:

"'Pardon, Senor, but I am Joaquin and I have come to look at my head.'

"Before I could reply, he bowed and seemed to melt away into the night. Since that first meeting I have seen him several times, always late at night and he always says the same thing—'I am Joaquin and I have come to look at my head.'"

Now, before you jump to the conclusion that Mr. X had been sitting too long with the spirits, pause and consider some historical facts.

Hanging in the lobby is one of the Club's most prized possessions, one of California's most historical paintings, an oil study of Joaquin Murrieta, painted by one of the West's greatest artists, Charles Christian Nahl, sometime in the 1860s.

Now Nahl never saw Joaquin Murrieta, the bandit who terrorized California from 1850 until he was slain by a posse in the Gabilan Mountains, not far from Coalinga, in 1853.

But Nahl knew many of the men who had known Murrieta, knew members of the posse who trapped him, shot him, then cut off his head and returned it pickled in whisky that they might prove they had killed him and claim the reward of $6,000.

Nahl also saw the head of Joaquin, which was sold for $36 and placed on display around the state for many years, and was finally burned in the fire of 1906.

Mr. X's story of Joaquin desiring to look at his missing head has some verification in a story told many years ago by Bill Henderson, one of the Rangers in the posse that finally killed Joaquin and his chief lieutenant, Three-fingered Jack.

"I was riding in the outskirts of Los Angeles at dusk," Henderson recalled, "when a headless horseman, wrapped in a black serape rode up to me.

"I reached for my gun and demanded who he was and what he wanted. He replied, 'I am Joaquin and I want my head. I can have no peace until I get my head back.'

"It was only after I assured him that I did not have his head and did not know where it was that he spurred his horse and vanished into the darkness."

There are others who claim to have seen the headless horseman. Cowboys and hunters who have gone into the lonely Arroyo Cantova, where Joaquin lost his head, claim they have seen the powerful black horse with the headless rider.

But on the other hand, to disprove Mr. X's contention that he has seen Joaquin gazing at his own portrait, there are those who claim Joaquin never was killed.

It should be remembered, however, that there are always such tales. There was the story that John Wilkes Booth, the assassin of President Lincoln, was not killed in a barn in southern Maryland but that he escaped and lived for many years. There are those today who maintain that Hitler did not commit suicide in his bunker in Berlin but that he escaped and is hiding out in South America.

The story that Joaquin Murrieta was not killed started shortly after the reward money was paid. There were five "Joaquins" in the gang, it was claimed and it was another Joaquin who was killed.

It is true there were five Joaquins. In addition to Murrieta there were Joaquin Carrillo, Joaquin Valenzuela, Joaquin Ocomorenia and Joaquin Botilleras, and it was one of these, some hold, who died in the lonely Arroyo Cantova in July 1853.

Joaquin, they say, escaped to Mexico, where he had sent much of the gold he looted, purchased a large ranch and lived in comfort until his death in 1879.

Joaquin Murrieta had a sister who lived in Marysville. She was shown the head and identified it as her brother. But some contend that under a pledge of secrecy she told close friends that it was not her brother's head.

And there have been stories of a mysterious Mexican digging at night in places where Joaquin had buried the plundered gold. And only Joaquin knew where the treasure was buried.

Certain it is, that none of the gold—reputedly valued in the millions—has ever been found by any of the thousands who have searched for it.

Since Mr. X's Joaquin only appears on foggy nights, I asked him if he had been reading Richard Harding Davis' thriller "In the Fog."[1] He admitted being familiar

---

1. Richard Harding Davis (1864–1916) was a writer and journalist best known for his reporting on the Spanish-American War. His fictional story "In the Fog," published in 1901, tells of an American in London who leaves a private club on the night of the "Great Fog" in 1897 and stumbles across some murder victims. Perhaps the Press Club had a copy of "In the Fog" in its library.

with that book, but denies that it had any connection with his seeing Joaquin.

So the question is—Does Mr. X see Joaquin after a spirited evening? Or does the Press Club really have a ghost?

What do YOU think?

This article appeared in the 1964 issue of Scoop, *the San Francisco Press Club's annual magazine. The Press Club, which was founded in 1887, recently folded. It was located at 555 Post Street for many years, including when this article was written.*

Index

About the Editor

A resident of San Francisco for over 30 years, Rand Richards is a San Francisco historian and the author of two local best-selling books: *Historic San Francisco: A Concise History and Guide* and *Historic Walks in San Francisco:18 Trails Through the City's Past.* He is currently at work on a book about San Francisco during the Gold Rush.